December Grace

Embracing God's Strength in Seasons of Grief

Darlene R. Gildersleeve

Table of Contents

Acknowledgments *9*
Prologue *11*

Chapter 1 15
Chapter 2 19
Chapter 3 23
Chapter 4 27
Chapter 5 31
Chapter 6 37
Chapter 7 41
Chapter 8 43
Chapter 9 49
Chapter 10 53
Chapter 11 57
Chapter 12 61
Chapter 13 65
Chapter 14 69

Chapter 15 75
Chapter 16 79
Chapter 17 85
Chapter 18 87
Chapter 19 91

To Help *95*
Victim's Resources *97*
See Something, Say Something *99*
Grief Resources *101*
Word from the Author:
  The Story Behind the Book *103*
Word from the Author:
  A Personal Reflection on Grief *109*
Grief Discussion Questions *111*
About the Author .... *113.*

© 2024, Darlene R. Gildersleeve
December Grace: Embracing God's Strength in Seasons of Grief

All rights reserved. No part of this publication may be reproduced, distributed, or transmitted in any form by any means, including photocopying, recording, or other electronic methods without the prior written permission of the author, except in the case of brief quotations embodied in reviews and certain other noncommercial uses permitted by copyright law. For permission requests, write to the author at the address below.

All Scripture quotations, unless otherwise indicated, are taken from the Holy Bible, New International Version®, NIV®. Copyright ©1973, 1978, 1984, 2011 by Biblica, Inc.™ Used by permission of Zondervan. All rights reserved worldwide. www.zondervan.comThe "NIV" and "New International Version" are trademarks registered in the United States Patent and Trademark Office by Biblica, Inc.™

ISBN: 979-8-9911328-5-5

Printed in the United States of America

First Printing, 2024.

*To my loving parents—
Ned and Ella Mae Burkett, who shone love and healing
through a traumatic journey.*

acknowledgments

I want to thank God most of all, because without his direction and guidance in my life, I wouldn't have been able to do this.

Thank you to my loving husband, Matthew, who was my rock! He walked beside me through the ups and downs of this journey. Thanks for always making me feel loved, cared for, and special. Thank you to my two children, Rachel and Ryan, for your unconditional love. And Rachel, for your talented editing skills!

To my precious mother, Ella Mae, who has remained my steadfast love throughout all these years, I love you!!

To my two cherished high school friends, Heather and Rhonda. You both walked beside me, listened to my pain, held my hand, and encouraged me to keep on going without saying a word. I cannot love you two enough!

A special thank you to my college roommates, Lisa and Tina. You both were my "no matter what" friends. You loved me no matter what. I could call you "no matter what" any time of the day or night. I could vent to you "no matter what" and I didn't have to explain myself "no matter what." I sure cherish our friendship.

To Marla, who was my spiritual mentor and walked me through the healing process. She was the calmness in my storm and continued to love me!

Thanks to Paula for the added laughter that I needed along the journey of this book. And especially for the awesome book title that came to be through miscommunication!

Sandy, who continued to pray for me and the added necessary humor when needed.

Thank you to Joann, my second mother, who has been my constant rock in my life and the stability I needed throughout this journey.

Helen, for her constant love and strength that she extended towards me when I was struggling.

Thank you to a few other special friends (you know who you are). You all have been an anchor in my life and such encouragers along the way. You listened to me, gave amazing advice, and allowed me to cry anytime, whether it was over the phone or in their work office. In the famous words of George Bailey, "No man is a failure who has friends." I am so thankful for those special friends!

Joelle (Joelle Watt Braid photography), your story is a beautiful one just waiting to be told! God placed you in my life because he knew the bigger story!!! Valla for your amazing talent on my face! You both are so talented in pulling my inner beauty outward. You two are the BEST!

Amy, for her wise words of spiritual guidance and for always accepting me without any judgment! Thank you for opening up your beautiful backyard, especially your garden. A Christian sister for sure!

To my editor and publisher, Katie, who was the true inspiration to show me that I can do this. Morgan, for her continued pursuit in this case—you were a pivotal person who got the wheels in motion and kept Marcia's story alive.

prologue

Ned Burkett was six years older than Ella Mae when they met in college in Rochester, New York, on a warm August day in 1959. After just one date, the couple had fallen madly in love.

Ned, studying in the School of Divinity, was determined to make his father proud. Ella Mae, bitten by the American Dream, was eager to start a family and her career as a businesswoman. The more time Ned and Ella Mae spent together, the more their love blossomed. They dreamed of being married, having four children, and living humble, God-fearing lives complete with a white picket fence.

Just a year after meeting, Ned and Ella Mae were married on August twenty-seventh. They passed their college experience together in marital bliss. Upon graduating, Ella Mae was expecting their first child—a son named Dale, who came into the world with a sharp cry.

Ned was simultaneously being placed as pastor over his first congregation in Sugar Grove, Pennsylvania.

Ned pastored at his first church for a few years before the council moved him to a new church in Warren, Pennsylvania. Ella Mae packed up the house in boxes with color-coded labels between nursing and chasing a busy toddler around.

When the Burkett family arrived in Warren, they began settling into a new routine. A few months after arriving, Ella Mae was expecting again. They prayed for a little girl and hoped she would become the perfect companion to their three-year-old son.

Marcia's arrival into their world was a touch more chaotic than Dale's—a telling sign of what was to come with their strong-willed little lady.

The family adjusted and fell into a new normal. With Dale in preschool, Ella Mae was able to focus all her attention on Marcia. She was a picture-perfect, doting mother. Ella Mae had put growing her career on the back burner until Marcia was a little older.

But it wasn't long before Ella Mae was expecting their third child. Two years later, the Burkett family found out they were growing by one. Darlene came into the world with a burst of joy. Ned and Ella Mae were elated to share their love with another baby girl. Their dreams of having four children, though, were dashed after Darlene was born. She was a sickly child, and juggling three children and a ministry was far tougher than expected.

While their family felt complete, they started to feel the setting wasn't quite right for their ministry. Just after Darlene was born, the Burketts moved once more to Fleming, Pennsylvania.

As they unpacked the car, Ned had a feeling of stability, knowing they'd be there for a while. The children grew up together and quickly learned their roles in the family at the new home as the pastor's kids. Ella Mae became a bit more strict and stern in order to juggle her kids and ministry as the pastor's wife, but the children always knew they were loved deeply.

After settling into Fleming for a few years, Ned brought home a gift for the kids. Taffy, a white French poodle, bounded up the stairs with much excitement for her new home. The kids squealed and embraced their newest family member.

Ned continued to minister to his congregation and found connections in the strangest places. It wasn't odd for Ella Mae to have to hunt him down in the grocery store after he wandered away, only to find him a few aisles over talking and praying for someone new.

Ned had a way about him that made others lower their guard and open up. He was always willing, no matter the day or hour, to make time for the needs of others. He was a pastor in the truest sense of the word. Ned came home each evening from days filled with counseling, hospital visits, elderly care runs, and sermon writing. And his wife was a pastor's wife in the sweetest definition. She dutifully served in Sunday School, helped with Wednesday night Bible study, and hosted Vacation Bible School in the summer.

The family lived a life of relative normalcy, with all of the expected hangups as the kids grew up. As time went by, the children began to find their footing in the small town of Fleming.

Fourteen years after moving to their new town, the Burkett family had a house full of teenagers. Naturally, the teens went through a rebellious phase. In the midst of this season, an unthinkable tragedy occurred. The family had to navigate the sudden loss of their oldest daughter, Marcia.

chapter 1

"I know this is going to sound crazy, Darlene, but I think this is what I was meant to do."

Ten minutes ago, my phone lit up with a call from Morgan, the daughter of a family friend. Her caller ID was backed by a photo of her and Maverick, her massive Newfoundland, sitting atop a fourteener in Colorado. Her bright, beaming smile rivaled the view of the peaks in the background.

Morgan wasn't related to us by blood, but since my mother babysat her mom over the years, it wound our families together inextricably.

Sitting in my car outside the cafe, I drummed my fingers on the steering wheel. Morgan's call was anything but social. I had come to look forward to her random check-ins, hoping when I saw her face fill my screen to hear about her latest excursion or solo hiking trip.

"I'm just not sure, Morgan," I said at last, tugging on my earring. "Marcia has been gone a long time. I'm not sure reopening her case is the best idea."

"Just promise me you'll think about it? I haven't been able to stop thinking about Marcia's story since my Nana told me what happened. I've got connections now that I'm done with school, and I think we could get the gears turning again."

I glanced in my rearview mirror; I had been parked in a drop-off lane for twenty minutes longer than expected, and I was waiting to see a meter maid come around the corner and tell me to leave. It would be an easy out of this conversation. One I desperately craved.

But instead, I saw my sister's eyes looking back at me. Blue eyes with a burst of icy glaciers in the center. The corners dubbed down ever so slightly under a thick brush of dark lashes. She had eyes like Marilyn Monroe's. Movie star eyes are what everyone said. In one glance, they fluttered innocently, and in another, they charred you to the core with their intensity.

I blinked, and she was gone. My hazel brown eyes were filled to the water line, and shiny tears were peering back at me.

"What do you say?" The hope in Morgan's voice found the crack in my heart, and a thin stream of tears worked its way down my cheek.

"I'll think about it," I said with a deep breath, releasing my grip from the steering wheel. When had my finger drumming turned into a death grip? Perhaps we weren't ready for this—perhaps I wasn't ready for this.

※

"Hurry up, they're waiting for us!" I raced to zip up my bright pink winter coat and tugged on my waterproof snow boots. Marcia was taking forever to get her snow clothes on.

I wondered if she was as slow as molasses or if she was simply uninterested in spending time with the other neighbor kids. Marcia spent a lot of time to herself; I didn't understand the lure of it. While she would run to her room after school to be alone, I would change into play clothes and head outside.

"Come on, come on," I begged her with one hand already on the door handle. It was the first snowfall of the year, and I was dying to try out my new Christmas bobsled. The bright red metal sled was fastest on icy snow days like today. I was buzzing with excitement to try it out. Marcia was slowly buttoning her snow pants over long johns. I groaned. "What's taking so long? Just put your shoes and coat on!"

Marcia's only response was a withering look as she trudged slowly across the kitchen to the closet.

I crossed my arms over my chest and let out an annoyed sigh. She always did this. Even though she was two years older than me, she didn't like making friends, and that ruined my chances at making friends also. I couldn't go outside without her and she knew it.

Finally, after ten excruciatingly long minutes, we were dressed and out the door. I galloped ahead to the side of the house to collect the bobsled. We lived in the small town of Fleming, Pennsylvania, where everyone knew everyone. We were going to meet the neighbor kids at the hill across from the railroad tracks—the best hill in town for sledding. I had never ridden a real bobsled before and could scarcely contain my excitement.

Marcia sulked behind me at a snail's pace, but I was determined not to let her get to me. The sky was blue, the snow was deep, and our friends were waiting. We had two days left of Christmas vacation before going back to school. That meant two full days of sledding, eating cookies, and watching old reruns on our family room television.

Within minutes, Marcia and I and the gang of neighbor kids stood at the top of the hill. We took turns riding to the bottom, hooping and hollering. At eleven years old, I was sure that life couldn't get any better than this.

As dusk came quickly, the precipitation fell harder, blurring our vision. Marcia was ready to go home an hour ago and had already begun walking away as I whined.

"Just one more? Please, please, please, pleeeeeease?" Marcia stopped to look back at me. She had barely talked to any of the neighbor kids during sled riding. It's like she didn't want to have fun.

"Yeah, Marcia, come on, let's go one more time," our neighbor, Jimmy, coaxed. To which she turned and crossed her arms.

She wasn't going to ride with me, but she wouldn't leave without me either. That was good enough for me. The snow had turned to sleet, and as I saddled up on the sled, I tugged my hat down over my eyes and let Jimmy give me a big push.

Two days later, I woke up in the hospital. They told me I had sustained a bruised liver and lungs and was bleeding internally. My metal bobsled hit a patch of ice, and I slid off only to be met with a fire hydrant. The impact rendered me unconscious. I owe my life to Marcia. Between her and the other neighbor kids, they managed to get me home and get help quickly.

I spent three weeks in the hospital. Mom, Dad, Dale, and Marcia took turns staying by my side. When I finally returned home, Marcia tended to me, bringing me food and drink when I needed it and completing my chores in my stead.

She didn't say much, but her presence was enough. When the Tylenol wore off, she was a strong, calming force at my side.

One day, when the pain was particularly difficult to resolve, Marcia held my hand and looked into my eyes. Those deep blue eyes pierced my heart and showered me with intensity. "You're going to be all right."

Her certainty was the only assurance I needed.

Later that week, the newspaper published a note from my father thanking God for healing me and all the emergency personnel who helped save his little girl.

☙

It had been five days since Morgan's call, and I couldn't stop replaying it in my head. *I think this is what I was meant to do.* What if she was right? Could this be God's answer to our family's prayer? Marcia had been gone for thirty-three years now. The pain of it all was a tide barely held at bay. The faint hint of her memory could send my mother into a depressive episode.

When kind churchgoers would ask after her, my mother's once-sunshiney countenance would darken, and she'd walk away wordless. The mention of my sister had caused her so much grief over the years, reopening a scabbed wound time and again. No matter how my father and I tried to mitigate the loss, there was no getting around the vacuum her absence created. How could I put my mother through that again?

Now, thirty-three years removed from the initial incident, we finally had a semblance of peace. Mom and Dad have found ways to busy themselves, to hold the pain at arm's length for most days. I had thrown myself into school then work and building my own family.

What if Morgan dug into Marcia's cold case and uprooted all that we laid to rest? Would it change everything?

But what if Morgan uncovered the truth of what really happened? What if Morgan's connections with local PD had the answers we could never reach? I had to try.

For Marcia's sake, I needed to try.

That night, I sat down and opened my journal.

Dear God,

I don't think I can face this pain again. I don't think I can go through it all again… remembering it all after trying so hard to push it away. God, I feel so guilty wanting to forget. It's not that I want to forget my sister, but without any real answers, what else can I do? Please help me, please give me strength. Will you show me what to do? I can't do this without you.

In Jesus' Name,
Amen

"But he said to me, 'My grace is sufficient for you, for my power is made perfect in weakness.' Therefore, I will boast all the more gladly about my weaknesses so that Christ's power may rest on me. That is why, for Christ's sake, I delight in weaknesses, in insults, in hardships, in persecutions, in difficulties. For when I am weak, then I am strong."

2 Corinthians 12:9-10

chapter 2

"So, what would it look like if I gave you my go-ahead? To, you know, look into what happened with Marcia?" I stood looking out the window above my kitchen sink, phone crooked on my shoulder. Our house backed up against a line of trees. It reminded me of my parents' homestead, where they've retired. Beyond the line of trees was the lake. Growing up, I had always wished we lived near a lake so we could swim in the hot summers. I was grateful to be living out the prayers of my youth.

"I'd like to start at the beginning. I only know your family's story from my mom, and I'd like to get your account of what happened. I'll be in town visiting my grandmother. Why don't we start there?"

And then what? What happens then? I wanted to scream. Once I had accepted the idea of letting another person in on the mystery surrounding my sister, I knew I was opening my heart to the possibility of searing pain all over again. The sheer hint of this degree of vulnerability made it difficult to keep my emotions in check.

But I didn't scream. I held my breath until the feeling passed. Shutting my eyes tight, I conjured the picture of Morgan from my caller ID.

Strong-willed, mountain-climbing Morgan.

She was trying to help. She wanted to find the truth as much as we did.

"Let's start there."

☙

We walked to the bus stop everyday from kindergarten until junior year. Our school was just three streets away, separated from our house by a small two-lane intersection that didn't require a crosswalk. We would pass Old Man Montgomery's hardware store and the Fleming Post Office on the corner.

In the morning, I tried to chat my sister up, but she never perked—only giving me dull murmurs as replies to my bubbling chatter. I had wanted nothing more than a closeness with my sister, but my every attempt was met with stone-cold silence. Over time, I stopped trying as hard. I let her silence envelop me, too, and I refrained from my usual chirping in the morning, finding a sacred peace in our silent walks to school. It wasn't my preference, but I accepted it.

Once school let out, there was no holding back. By the time our afternoon walk rolled around, I already had the opportunity to be social for eight glorious hours. My social meter was overflowing and there was no escaping it.

For Marcia, she seemed even more withdrawn by the final bell. I think Marcia thrived in solitude and privacy. It was like her time around other people sucked the marrow from her bones, leaving her more hollow than before.

In the years since my sled riding accident, I hoped we would grow closer together. That her "hero moment" to my "victim experience" would bond us as sisters. I envisioned us sharing clothes and makeup, talking about boys, and staying up late gossiping. But the chasm between our striking personality differences only grew wider.

On this particular walk to the bus stop, we were closely followed by John, a boy in the grade between Marcia and me. Marcia had just gotten her hair cut, and it wasn't as nearly as flattering as the one she had previously.

John began taunting us and lobbing snowballs at our backs. I watched as Marcia flinched but said nothing. She trudged slowly towards home in her usual tortoise-like pace. *Splat, splat.* The wet sound of snowballs landing on Marcia's backpack continued.

Each subsequent round of hits agitated me further.

"Why don't you say something?" I hissed at her.

Marcia grunted a halfhearted *meh*.

I slapped my hands against my jeans; she was being ridiculous. Her listlessness was unrealistic. She was the older sibling, and this kid was just some punk—she could easily turn around and make him stop.

The next snowball was so large that its shrapnel bounced off Marcia and hit me.

"That's it, if you're not going to do something, *then I will*," I spat at Marcia through ground teeth before whirling around and throwing my backpack on the ground.

"That's enough, John!" I yelled as I scooped down to pack the perfect snowball.

"What are you doing, Darlene?" My sister's quiet voice came from over my shoulder, but I paid her no mind. I was already keyed up from John's pestering. I was not about to let this rascal treat us this way and get away with it.

"Leave. My. Sister. *Alone*!" The snowball hurled through the air and landed squarely in John's face—the most satisfying crunch, followed by his boyish howl, spelled out victory for me.

I spun to high-five my sister, but she wore a face of horror.

"*Oh my gosh!* What did you just do? You *broke* his glasses, Darlene!" She stood away from me like I was some dangerous monster. John ran home crying, holding his glasses to his face.

"I don't understand. I did what had to be done. What *you* should have done." Shaking my head, I grabbed my backpack and pushed past her. Was she kidding? Was Marcia really mad at *me*? I had just protected her; I thought she would be glad I stood up for her.

After dinner that night, our home phone rang. I watched my father cross from where he sat, reading the paper to pick up the rotary phone. He bunched the cord around his fist, flexing his fingers as he listened. He hung up quietly and strode into the living room where we sat on the floor doing homework during the evening news.

"That was John's mom. You girls want to tell me what happened?" Our father was not an intimidating man. He was kind and soft-spoken. We far more feared his disappointment than wrath.

Dropping my pencil, I looked at Marcia, whose empty eyes stayed fixed on her workbook.

"Hm?" My father's first warning came in the tune of a question.

"It was me," I said at last. "I did it. John was making fun of Marcia and me and throwing snowballs at her. So I threw one back at him." I chewed my bottom lip.

"Is that what happened, Marcia?"

Marcia didn't reply.

"I swear it, Dad. John's a rascal. He deserved it."

Marcia closed her book and got up at an unnaturally quick rate. She went straight to her room and didn't come out until morning.

☙

Marcia never stood up to John or any of the other kids at school; I never understood that. Now, I catch myself wondering if she didn't stand up to whoever took her from us.

Lord,
I know these what-ifs aren't helpful. Help me to let go of the past and move forward. Please take these memories from me and let them rest. I just want to move on.
In Jesus Name,
Amen

chapter 3

Morgan rustled in her tote for a moment before extracting an old school tape recorder. She placed it on the wooden picnic table top between us.

I eyed it surreptitiously, doubt beginning to gather into a nervous knot in my stomach. Was this really a good idea? What can a newly graduated private investigator do that aged cops can't? Below the table, my hands made fists, and my nails dug into the fatty part of my palm.

"Ready?" The sparks of fresh fervor in her eyes wilted my fears just a bit. I was most certainly not ready, but I didn't think I ever would be.

I gave Morgan a curt nod, and she reached out to press the record button.

"I am recording our conversation so that I can keep all the facts straight and gather information from all reliable sources. Do you understand?"

I nod once again.

"Can I have your verbal consent?"

"Yes," I gulped so loudly I'm sure the recorder picked it up.

"Today is July 20th, 2020. Can you state your name for the record?"

I blinked as the summer breeze blew past us, forcing wisps from my ponytail to flutter across my face and into my eyes. "Darlene Gildersleeve," I said, reaching up to slide pieces of my hair behind my ears.

Gildersleeve. I had been married for more than twenty years. I had officially been with my husband longer than the time I had with my sister. The thought struck a chill through me. The unease was creeping back in.

"When was the last time you saw your sister?"

"The summer of 1986."

"Can you tell me more about what was happening at that time?"

&

"Honey, the Reardons will be here any minute," Mother's voice bounced down the small hallway from the kitchen into my room. The Reardons were friends of the family, and their only daughter, Paula, was Marcia's age. Paula was arguably one of the only friends I ever witnessed Marcia making.

I sat in front of my mirror, smoothing my hair into perfect plaits, getting ready for dinner. Next door, Marcia's room was quiet. But that hadn't been unusual. Marcia had always preferred her privacy and alone time, even when we shared the purple room back in the small town we grew up in.

But ever since our father was assigned to a new church to pastor in Philipsburg, Marcia only became more reticent. She got her own room since the parsonage was bigger than the last. Our older brother always had a room to himself, while we girls typically shared. This was the first time we each had our own personal space. I thought it would have made her happier—she'd get loads of alone time. I thought not having to share would make her want to spend time together, but I was wrong.

The only time I heard her door creak open was late at night after everyone was already in bed or early in the morning when only my father was awake.

She had become a nocturnal owl. Sometimes, I heard my parents whisper their concerns when they thought I wasn't listening.

Nancy, one of the ladies in our father's congregation, had rung Mom the other night to let her know she saw Marcia wandering down the back country road alone at night.

Reckless, dangerous behavior, I heard Mom say.

Marcia was seventeen now—a woman, Daddy would say as though that made her activities typical. I was frightened for my sister. She hadn't found anyone to get along with, not like I had. It seemed anytime I brought my friends around, they would fawn over Marcia. They wanted her to like them. It made me spitting mad. She didn't care, though; I had never even seen her try to make friends or accept their admiration. I wondered if she was alone because she wanted to be or because she thought no one was good enough for her.

I finished tying braids in my hair and went to Marcia's room.

"*Knock, knock,*" I said in an exaggerated tone before letting myself into her room.

Marcia sat at her desk at the far side of the room. She scowled at me over her shoulder. "I hate when you do that."

I rolled my eyes and hopped onto her bed. Fashion sketches were all around her room. Drawings of models wearing everything from gowns and professional suits to skimpy bathing suits. I marveled at her handiwork.

In the corner of her room stood a rack of shelves with material on it. Denim, cotton, linen, stacked upon each other. On another shelf were spools of colored thread, and various sized needles.

Stopping at Marcia's desk where she sat was a Singer sewing machine. Our parents let us use our grandmother's since she had shown such an interest in making clothes. The machine was an heirloom and beat out a rhythmic sound as she finished a line of stitches.

"Mom said it's time." I eased off the bed toward her. Peering over her shoulder, I saw she was fashioning something denim.

"It's crazy how you've been doing that since we were little," I reminisced fondly. "Remember when you used to make my Barbies their own designer jeans?" The memory of her measuring my itty bitty Barbies to make them clothes warmed my chest and brought a chuckle forth.

Marcia acted as though I didn't say anything; I just yanked the fabric from the machine to examine it closely before turning it and sliding it back under the needle.

Her ignorance stung, a slap of rejection.

"Come on, or we're gonna be in trouble." I straightened up and headed for the door.

"I'll be there in a minute," she murmured with pins between her lips.

The Reardon family arrived, and my hostess of a mother threw open the door as if the president was joining us for dinner. She lavishly gestured to the dining room where a Sunday feast was already waiting.

My mother floated around the dining room in her beige, belted dress, serving us our meal. My father, the pastor, sat at the head of the table, chatting with Mr. Reardon on his right. His wife, Mrs. Reardon, sat next to him with her daughter, Paula, just across from her.

I sat on one side of Paula, near my mother, and my sister sat on the other, next to our father. Our brother was working and managed to get out of this dinner, leaving one seat vacant at our dining room table. Lucky.

When my mother finished serving everyone, she sat at the end of the table opposite our father. We held hands to say grace, and when I peeked, I noticed Marcia hadn't closed her eyes or bowed her head. How long had she been doing that?

I kept one eye closed and one eye on her until my father was done; her gaze was fixed on the plate of meatloaf and potatoes. We finished praying, and mild dinner chatter filled the room.

After the plates were cleared and Mr. Reardon and our Father were all done, Mr. Reardon turned his gaze to Marcia.

"So, what are your plans after school, Miss Marcia?"

"I want to move to Atlanta, Georgia, or LA."

Mom audibly sucked in a sharp inhale.

If Mr. Reardon was surprised, he didn't show it. He smiled warmly. "What for? That's an awfully big change for a young woman like yourself."

"There's an important fashion school there," Marcia replied unabashedly.

I looked at my mother, who guffawed at my father.

"Oh, I see. We have friends in Atlanta. Maybe we could introduce you—"

"What's Atlanta like, Mr. Reardon?"

"Marcia," my father chuckled in surprise and laid a hand gently on her arm, "now's not the time for this conversation. Let the man eat his dessert." His comment rippled through the uneasy tension in the room. But Marcia's eyes were unwavering.

"It's all right, Ned. She's just curious, I imagine," Mr. Reardon said to my father. "Well, I've only ever visited during summer vacation, but it's a large, bustling place," he said now to Marcia.

She nodded for him to continue. He picked up his spoon to scoop up some berry pie. Mom had spent all afternoon fretting around the kitchen to make sure everything would be just right for this evening.

"It's the hub of rock 'n' roll right now, they say. Not exactly the best place for a girl like you." He gestured to Marcia and chewed on the pie.

"Well, it doesn't matter. I'm going to move there when I graduate."

My mother's fork clattered to the plate, and I couldn't help but lurch past Paula to gape at my sister. This took us all by surprise.

"*Marcia*," my mother said through a thin line of a smile, "you never mentioned this before?"

Even I understood that was Mom's polite way of telling her to shut up. Marcia either missed the social cue or didn't care.

She showed zero expression as she turned her gaze back on Mr. Reardon. "So you don't live in Atlanta, but you said you know someone who does? Could you get me connected?"

"Marcia," Mother hissed.

Mr. Reardon shot my father a wary look. I always thought Marcia was sort of *backward*, but now this proved it. She was way out of line being so forthcoming, and she had no idea.

"We'll talk after dinner," my father commanded with a note of finality.

The rest of dinner was bogged down with the earlier tension, although you wouldn't have guessed it by way of Mr. Reardon and my father's discourse. They were old chums with much to catch up about.

The tension built until it was officially *after dinner*. Marcia's eyes were intensely focused on the Reardon's. She looked like a wild cat looking to pounce on its prey.

My mother saw the predatory glint in her eyes and headed it off. "Marcia, help me clean up dinner."

Marcia gritted her teeth. I had never seen my sister seem so… expressive before. It was unnerving.

My mother managed to keep Marcia away from the Reardons for the rest of the evening. It wasn't until after my mother waved goodbye from the porch that the real fuss began.

Marcia stormed out of her room, slamming the door behind her. Against my sleuthing wishes, my father ushered me into mine. From the safety of my room, I placed an ear to the door and listened.

"It's either London, LA, or Georgia." Her voice was muffled through the door but loud enough to be clear.

"I'm not staying here any longer. I can't take it."

There was a pause, where my parents responded, but their voices were too low to be heard.

After a few quiet minutes, a door slammed shut. The front door, I thought. Then the door across from mine quietly snicked closed—my parent's room.

She left.

chapter 4

Morgan cleared her throat as she shifted in her seat. She tossed her long hair over one shoulder and squared up to the table.

"Darlene, I can't imagine how hard this must be to rehash, but anything you can tell me will help me find out what happened to your sister." She leaned onto the picnic table, elbows flat against the wood.

"I'm sorry, what?" It was too easy to get caught in the flood of memories once they began.

"When was the last time you saw your sister? Can you tell me about it?"

"Right." I pressed a clammy palm to my temple. "Marcia was upset. She wanted to go to Atlanta, Georgia, to some fashion program. My parents didn't want her to go, but she said she'd leave anyway. So my father reached out to some friends, the Reardons. They had a friend in Atlanta who could help Marcia get settled."

"You said this was 1986, right?"

I nodded.

In the distance, children's laughter and squeals filled the air. The nearby playground was home to many summer groups, and their joy made this conversation even more bittersweet.

"When did Marcia leave for Georgia?"

"She moved out in February, just before graduating. She got an apartment nearby and finished school. I didn't see her much after that. Then, shortly after summer break began, she moved to start the program in the fall." I paused, feeling the tears catching in my throat. Pulling the tissue from my pocket, I pressed it against my eyes and apologized.

"I didn't even get to say goodbye."

A sob ripped through me without permission.

Morgan offered me a new tissue from her bag with a gentle tut.

"You mean you never heard from her again?" Morgan's brow dipped in concern.

"My parents had, I'm sure." I pressed the clean tissue to my eyes again, cursing myself for wearing makeup to this meeting. "She would call once in a while, just to let them know she was okay. But she never asked for me when she'd call."

"Did your parents have anywhere to reach her?"

"No, it was the time before cell phones. We only had home phones and pay phones, and Marcia couldn't afford either."

"So she moved more than three thousand miles away without much money?"

"Our parents tried to stop her and tell her to wait and save up money, but she was so relentless when she made up her mind. So they tried to support her, but on a pastor's salary, it wasn't much. My mom cleaned houses sometimes to make up the difference, but it was a humble time." I lifted a shoulder, batting my glistening eyelashes.

"Did Marcia work while she was in Georgia?"

"Uh." I tried to remember. So many years had gone by. "Yeah, I think she waitressed, but she was going to school full-time." The fact that I couldn't remember this simple detail ate at me. How did I not know whether my sister worked while in Georgia? That information would have been vital to an investigation.

"She was?" she asked in surprise. "I wasn't sure if she made it into the school. What was the school called?"

The pang of guilt and frustration churned deeper.

"I don't know," I heaved a sigh. "Oh gosh, that's terrible, isn't it? I can't believe I don't know."

My head sank into my hands as I let the tears fall.

Click. Morgan turned the recorder off.

"Darlene, it's not your fault. You were only sixteen years old when she went missing. Besides, grief does strange things to our memory. I've seen it firsthand, and I'm sure you've felt it. We'll find the information another way."

I thought about what she said. Her warm brown eyes felt like a comforting cup of cocoa. I took a shuddering breath to calm my cries, and another memory bobbed to the surface of my mind, drawing me back.

☙

"*Mo-om!*" Marcia yelled from the living room. "How does this thing work?"

Marcia stood in the middle of the room, smacking a large, clunky remote off her palm. She pointed it at the television and jammed her fingers into the buttons, grunting in frustration as nothing happened.

Pillows and blankets lay spread across the floor, the perfect slumber party set up for Marcia's fifteenth birthday. Mom stepped gingerly between them and reached out for the remote in Marcia's hands. I sat perched on the edge of the couch in my pajamas, watching as they tried to learn to use the VCR we rented for the weekend.

Marcia was allowed to invite a couple of girls from school to stay the night. She invited Paula, Patti, Rhonda, Heather, and Theresa. I grumbled when I found out. Patti, Rhonda, and Theresa were my friends first. Marcia had an annoying habit of stealing my friends. I thought because she was older, she wouldn't have any trouble making friends. But for some reason, she struggled. The only friends she made were the ones I brought around or the kids of our parent's friends.

I looked at the clock and realized they'd be here soon. Mom had been rushing around the kitchen getting food and snacks ready for their arrival until now. Marcia groaned in impatience at the remote. I watched as my mother threw up her hands, giving up.

"Ned! Honey, we could use your help," Mom called as she quickly walked down the hallway to their bedroom, where he was resting after a long day of making pastoral visits.

"This stupid thing," Marcia muttered. Then she said to me, "This better not ruin the party!"

I slid off the arm of the couch onto the cushion and reached for the large VHS tape. I ran my fingers along the edges of the thick plastic cover. *The Outsiders*. I flipped it over to read the back cover.

"They grew up on the outside of society. They weren't looking for a fight. They were looking to belong."

My finger traced over the tagline. I knew this was a book we were going to read later in school, so I was excited to watch the movie. It was a big deal to see a movie, and even more so that our parents rented the VCR and a VHS tape for Marcia's birthday.

Our parents were protective of us and didn't let us watch many things. A twinge of jealousy shuddered through me. *I hope my parents do something like this for me when it's my fifteenth birthday…*

The doorbell chimed, and the first of our friends arrived. My mother had the kitchen counters lined with chips, dips, and snacks. She even splurged on soda. I milled about, grazing on the food, while Marcia greeted *her* friends. *My friends*, I thought bitterly.

The girls arrived one after the other, and after a round of pizza for dinner, it was time to cut the cake. We circled around Marcia at the dining room table, giggling in the dark as my mother lit the candles atop the chocolate cake she spent the afternoon baking.

Mom and Dad stood at the head of the table while Paula and Patti crowded in closest to Marcia, leaving me out. I felt second-rate in that moment—Marcia had stolen the show and my friends' affection in this glittering moment. With the lights off, I let the feeling of being overlooked wash over me, and I pouted. Rhonda and Heather crowed *happy birthday* over my shoulder, jarring me for a moment.

As Mom finished lighting the last candle, I looked up. She began to share her birthday blessings for Marcia, and I watched Marcia's eyes carefully. My initial thought was *she better be grateful for all this*. But from where I stood, I saw a flicker of shame and then true joy. Marcia looked at the cake and around at our friends as we sang to her.

She looked genuinely happy. Loved.

"She grew up on the outside of society. She wasn't looking for a fight. She was looking to belong."

And it hit me. My sister wasn't trying to steal my friends. Marcia wasn't looking for a fight. She just wanted to belong.

When the loud and off-pitch singing ended, my father flicked the lights back on, and Dale beat a hasty departure back to his room. Mom plucked the candles out of the cake and sliced it for each of us.

I slid around the table and hugged Marcia. "Happy birthday, Marcia."

Morgan's hand gently caressed mine, pulling it away from my face. She peeked up at me with compassion.

I spent so much energy as a kid fighting with my sister. So much time was lost to our quarrels and bickering. Time I would never get back. Grief was like a rock in my chest, pulling me down.

"I can't imagine what it's like to lose a sister, but to rehash it over again… without any certainty of truth? You are so brave." She emphasized her last statement by squeezing my hand.

I looked away. "I don't feel brave."

"You are. And you aren't alone. We are going to see what we can uncover together. Let's stop here. We've covered a lot. I'm going to reach out to the local PD in Gwinnett County to see if I can find the information for the detective who was on duty when her case came through. When I find that out, we can talk again. How's that sound?"

Relief flooded me.

I was more than ready to end the conversation for now. But more so, I was relieved someone else was taking the reins on finding out the truth. Our family had dug as much as our pain had allowed over the years. But in the end, there were only dead ends.

Dear God,

Only you know the truth of what happened to my sister. I pray you will bring the truth to light. Please help us find out what happened. Please guide the steps and decisions of Morgan and the police investigators involved. Help them find the evidence necessary to close the case. Bring what's been hidden to light. Shine your light on the darkness, and expose the truth. We can't do this without you. Please, God, please help. And Lord, please heal my heart. Heal the memories and help me to forgive myself…

In Jesus' Name,

Amen

"This is the verdict: Light has come into the world, but people loved darkness instead of light because their deeds were evil. Everyone who does evil hates the light and will not come into the light for fear that their deeds will be exposed. But whoever lives by the truth comes into the light, so that it may be seen plainly that what they have done has been done in the sight of God."

John 3:19-21

chapter 5

"Hey, I have some information for you. Do you have time to talk?"

The blue message bubble popped up on my Facebook Messenger app while I was at work. I sat back in the chair and stared at the message from Morgan.

"I've been in touch with the original detective on Marcia's case. I'm planning a trip to Georgia to go meet him and look at her case files."

I stared at the phone in my hand. It had been two weeks since the meeting with Morgan in the park. Life had returned to a somewhat regular pace, but the anger gnawing in the back of my mind never quieted. I knew from years of counseling that it wasn't really anger. It was the grief fighting for the attention I wouldn't give it.

My phone chimed again; it was another alert from Facebook.

"I need to get some more information about Marcia, the school she was attending, work, people she knew, etc. Do you think you could talk to your parents and see what you can learn from me?"

So this was really happening.

When Marcia first didn't come home, I hid myself in my room and refused to hear what my parents were saying. As time progressed, though, I couldn't face the fact that she would not be coming home.

I let the details blur past me. Intentionally forgetting the days as they passed. I didn't want to remember this pain; I didn't want it to seep into me and change me.

I chose denial.

The pain of knowing hurt worse than not knowing. The details stacked up like a monster growing inch by inch, becoming a looming shadow I couldn't outrun. Any details I learned had played over in my mind, eating me alive. I couldn't do it then. And now Morgan was asking me to open up my heart to look at the details.

I'm not sure I can do it, I thought as I clicked my phone's screen off.

The plaque on my door says I'm a therapist. The degrees on my wall say that I should know the process of grief. And I do. I've seen how it comes and goes at the least convenient of times, how it rockets through you in a range of emotions and leaves you feeling run over. Grief can bring people together, or it can tear them apart. Over the past decade, I have counseled hundreds of patients through their own personal losses and have seen the whole gambit of emotional responses. I should know how to deal with this.

But *knowing how* and *doing* are two very different things. In retrospect, I can see how the denial I chose as a teenager and young adult did more harm than good. I can acknowledge that processing my grief would have been better for me than the way I coped at the time.

Fighting the familiar itch to control everything in my world, I took a deep breath—as my own therapist had taught a younger me to do. My lungs filled and deflated as I let the intrusive thoughts pass. My eyes floated over my desk, and I reached out to reorient the pens and stapler into a perfect line and gathered the loose-leaf pages into a neat stack.

I chose denial then; I'm choosing healing now, I thought. Despite the creeping fear of slipping into old ways, I reopened my phone and typed out a quick message to Morgan.

"Anything you need. I'll do it for Marcia."

∞

"Darlene, come on, we never go out anymore," Matt groaned.

I shot him a look that told him not to press his luck.

"Escape is playing tonight, and you're gonna love them. They sound just like Journey." Matt circled his arms around me and pulled me close. "Everyone's gonna be there. Come on, it'll be totally cool."

Matt and I had been dating for a few months. We met through a mutual friend, Joann. I worked with her, and she was his mom's friend. When Matt's mom died, Joann made sure to always look after him. She was an angel and became his surrogate mom. I never met Matt's mom, but I knew Joann, and I respected her opinion very highly. When she introduced me to Matt, I wasn't sure. But I gave him a chance because of her.

Now, I was really falling for Matt. It took years for me to heal and get to a place where I could be in love, but I thought he might even be the one.

However, tonight, I was feeling off. I was on edge like something inside me wasn't quite settled. I didn't really want to be around people.

"Please, Rabbi? I—" Matt started, using his cute nickname for me.

"I just don't feel good, you know?" I said, not meeting his eyes.

"Come on." He stuck out his bottom lip in a dramatic pout that he knew would make me laugh.

"Okay, okay, fine! We'll go. Where is it?" I laughed and conceded. If it meant that much to him, I could handle myself out for one night.

"Up in Rossiter. Come on, I'll drive." He took my hand and led me out to the car, opening my door for me.

Thirty minutes later, we pulled into the parking lot of the Buffalo Lodge. I had to admit, the building did look cool. Matt was right—it would be a good night. I could put all the stress of work behind me and hang out for one night. I don't even know what was wrong with me anyway.

The DJ's music was thumping through the speakers and made my chest buzz. Matt made a beeline for drinks, and I slid onto a stool at a corner table. The band was still setting up, plugging cords into expensive-looking audio equipment, and rearranging guitars and drum materials.

A quick look around the room told me this was the spot to be tonight. People were filing in now by the tens, bringing with them the chilled night air. I tried to appreciate the breeze, knowing it would be packed, hot, and tight in here tonight. Laughter and greetings brightened the atmosphere despite the smoke machines attempting to dim the room.

On stage, a guy with a permed mullet did a sound check. He spun around and pointed to the light display. Someone off to the left of the stage hit the buttons to flick the lights on and off. It seemed like an impressive setup.

Matt dropped onto the stool next to me. "Sorry that took so long; I ran into some guys I knew. Mike and Vince."

He slid a glass of soda over to me, and I gazed past his shoulder. A group of girls my age shuffled in and went straight to the bar. I thought I recognized one of the girls but must have been mistaken.

"Let's get up close, huh?" Matt tugged my hand, and I followed him up to the stage when the band was gearing up to open.

The music started, and the light show began. Strobes of neon yellow, purple, and green crisscrossed the room. Cigarette smoke and the fog machine battled to claim the only fresh air around us.

Matt lifted his beer in cheer as the band opened with a Journey cover, "Any Way You Want It." They were good. I smiled at Matt and let the music in.

I am alive. I am allowed to have a good time, I told myself.

Halfway through their set, the crowd surged forward with a new wave of people trying to get closer to the stage. I turned with a cry as someone elbowed past me.

And that's when I saw her.

A few people away stood a girl dancing to the music. Her jet-black hair fell into her dark blue eyes, just like they always had. I could only see her profile, but I knew. Everything in me knew it was her.

It was Marcia.

I tore away from Matt and pressed into the crowd, weaving sideways. Shouts and shoves did nothing to stop me. I had to get to her. I needed to see her.

I knew she wasn't gone. I knew she wasn't in the grave.

My heart trumpeted in response. I reached out a hand to turn her around. Every ounce of denial that I struggled to overcome wiped me out at that moment.

When they buried the casket, I never saw her face. I never saw her! She couldn't be dead.

"Marcia!" I shouted over the music and pulled her to face me.

The woman who turned to look at me gave me a confused once-over. Her black hair was dark brown up close, and the blue eyes I thought I saw were actually green.

No, no, no. It couldn't be. It had to be Marcia. Marcia was here. Not gone.

My hand dropped. There were no words. I matched her bewildered look with one of my own. Somewhere in my quick jaunt, Matt must have noticed I was gone and found me because he rescued me just then.

But it was too late.

"Darlene?" He hollered over the music. "What's going on?" He looked from the girl before me to my quickly crumbling face.

I shook my head numbly and let him extricate me from the spot I had melted into. Even as we walked away, I felt a piece of me stay behind.

We slipped out of the overgrown crowd, and the numbness began to wear off. The heat in the small space made me nauseous.

"I need some air." I bolted out the door, feeling like I could throw up. I walked along the side of the log cabin lodge until I was far enough away from the music that I couldn't feel it reverberating inside my head anymore.

"Hey, hey," Matt called, trailing after me. "What's this all about?"

"No, no," I muttered to myself, squeezing my eyes shut. "It can't be."

I thought it was Marcia. That was Marcia, I thought to myself, holding back tears as best I could.

But I couldn't tell Matt. It hurt too much, saying it out loud. The sobs started. The ache in my chest that I had kept at bay cracked open wide and poured forth all the anger, fear, and pain I had been storing up.

"Oh, Rabbi, what is it?" Matt placed a consoling arm around me.

I know he was trying to help, but the anger of the grief came bubbling out of me.

I shoved away from him and turned to walk to the car. Wrapping my arms around myself, the tears kept coming.

It's not fair. I should be here with my sister. Why did this happen to me? This shouldn't have happened to me! I wailed silently to no one in particular. Maybe God, if he was listening.

Across the street, a store's marquee glowed with an Easter promotion. My heart sank, and I fell to my knees to catch my breath.

Easter was when we buried Marcia. Six years ago, on Easter. The emotions were too raw.

I'm sure I must have seen signs of the holiday coming—I must have somehow known subconsciously. I had been feeling off at work all week and unsettled, with my mind in a fog, not wanting to go out but not knowing why. And it never registered.

A strange peace settled over me. It was like my body knew what my heart was avoiding.

Marcia was gone, and my body wouldn't let me forget it.

Dear God,

When the memories come, hide me. Take me away and cover me with your wings. I don't want to feel all of these horrible emotions, but I know that in order to heal, I can't run from them. Please give me the strength to feel all the anger, fear, and pain. Stand by me so I don't have to do it alone. I know that if you're with me, I can do it. But I can't do it without you. Please help me to feel your nearness when the grief comes, when the memories come…

In Jesus' name,

Amen

"The LORD is close to the brokenhearted and saves those who are crushed in spirit."
Psalm 34:18

"He will cover you with his feathers, and under his wings, you will find refuge; his faithfulness will be your shield and rampart."
Psalm 91:4

chapter 6

"You never know what might be relevant in a cold case. Anything you can think of, any detail—no matter how minute—could be what cracks this thing wide open." Morgan did her best to reassure me when I got anxious talking about Marcia.

"Let's just go back to the beginning and tell me what happened as you remember it."

I took a deep breath. I have told and retold this account so many times that I could do it purely from memory without any hint of emotion. The therapist in me knew I was disconnecting my emotions, but I didn't mind. I couldn't be raw and visceral every time I spoke with Morgan; I might lose my mind.

"Marcia called one night in October, a few weeks before the holidays. I remember it was odd because Mom wasn't home, and Dad answered. He was tickled pink to talk to Marcia. She never really called just to talk but always had something to say or needed something." I let the image of Dad on the phone in the kitchen fill my mind. His smile was sincere and relaxed, and it made me relax, too, knowing nothing was wrong with Marcia this time.

"Was she in trouble a lot there? I mean, a young girl on her own in Atlanta in the 80s… There had to be some trouble, right?" Morgan questioned.

"Well, yes and no. She dropped out of school two weeks into the program and got a job as a waitress. So the call before this one was informing my parents of her recent, uh, *career change*."

"I see. They must have been so worried."

"They were. They insisted she come home, but she was stubborn. She refused to give up on the dream and wouldn't come back until she had something to show for it." I laughed under my breath, remembering how stubborn that girl could be.

☙

The steam rose from the plate my mother had just set before me. Roast beef and beets–*the worst*. I snuck a glance at Marcia; she hated beets even more than me. She was already glowering into the plate, and I groaned, knowing this dinner table was about to become a battlefield.

After my father said grace, I dug in. I plugged my nose and shoveled the beets down as quickly as possible. A nudge at the leg of my chair had me looking down. Our little French poodle, Taffy, peered up at me.

"No, girl, I don't think you'd even eat these." I crinkled my nose in disgust, and she yapped as if she completely understood me.

"Excuse me, young lady," Mother said, narrowing her gaze on me.

"Sorry," I went back to pushing the food around my plate until I worked up the courage again to plug my nose and finish the beets.

When my fork clattered onto the plate, a note of finality, I looked over to Marcia, who had barely touched her food. My mother followed my gaze and locked on Marcia.

"You better eat up," she said, spearing a chunk of beet.

"I hate beets. I'm not eating these!" Marcia pushed the plate away.

"Marcia, come on, just plug your nose like I did and eat them real quick."

"No! I'm not doing it!" She crossed her arms in defiance.

I looked across the table to Mother. She wasn't looking at Marcia, but I wasn't sure if it was because she wasn't tolerating her tantrum or because she was going to let it slide. I waited, and when our mother looked at Marcia, I could tell by the glint in her eyes that it was a deliberate pause.

"You will sit here at this table until you clear your plate." Mother didn't have to raise her voice to be scary—her tone was firm and gave me chills.

Marcia didn't reply but fixed her with a menacing glare in response.

A moment later, Father finished his dinner and stood from the table. I got up to follow him and took my plate to the kitchen.

From the kitchen, I could see Mother and Marcia squared off across the table from one another. It was like two generals at war.

"Who do you think will cave first?" I asked my Father as he rinsed off our plates, setting them in the sink.

He thought for a moment, then said, "Your sister came into this world stubborn from the day she was born. She came out of your mother with her fist raised." He looked like he wanted to say more, but he just shook his head in dismissal.

As we crossed through the dining room on the way to the living room, I whispered to Marcia, "Taffy won't eat the beets, so you're going to have to eat them. Just plug your nose. Don't be dumb!"

Marcia didn't bat an eyelash, just sat with stubborn arms crossed and mouth sewn shut.

All evening long, I would glance over my shoulder to find Marcia was still a permanent fixture at the table. Mother had moved on to clearing the kitchen but was always close enough to keep an eye on her.

I couldn't believe how strange she was acting. Didn't Marcia want to be free? Why couldn't she just surrender and eat the beets?

Eventually, nine o'clock rolled around, and it was bedtime. Marcia was sent to bed, and I listened around the corner as Mother scraped the food into the trash.

"I don't know what we're gonna do with that girl, Ned." Mother's whisper was almost drowned out by the sink's running water.

"We're doing our best. We just have to believe that God will work in her heart." Father moved toward the hallway, and I scurried back to my room.

I hoped he was right.

chapter 7

"So Marcia was a stubborn child?" Morgan mused after I shared that story over the phone.

"Yeah, a stubborn child who never broke. She became an even more rebellious teenager. My poor parents." My hand went to my brow, thinking about what my mother must have gone through while raising three kids. After Matt and I got married, we only had two kids, but having one less child than my parents didn't prevent me from feeling the challenges of raising strong personalities.

"How did her stubbornness affect those around her?"

"I don't know, but that's a great question. I guess she was insistent on doing things her way, and that often meant going against our parents' or teachers' rules. She tended to attract unsavory characters who acted the same way."

"Hmm, there could be something there. Did your parents look into her friends or the people she lived with in Georgia?"

"Yes, actually, her roommate. They were in touch with her a couple of times. She didn't seem like a bad apple. But we never knew who she was hanging out with. Marcia liked her privacy and wouldn't share much about her life, even if we pressed her for info.

"I'm actually really surprised she decided to come home." I paused, thinking of Marcia's blue eyes and how they set when she was determined to rebel against our parents. What must have changed her mind about coming home? "At the time, I was elated. She told Dad it was a secret and that she wanted to surprise Mom, but she needed money for the bus ticket."

"That was the call in October?" Morgan clarified.

"I watched my Father sit down in that instant and write a check and address an envelope. He promised it would be out in the mail first thing the next morning."

I could see the whole thing play out in my mind when Dad hung up the phone and swept into the living room, where I sat doing homework. He picked me up and hugged me. Marcia's coming home! he said.

"But she never got on that bus. We don't know if she got the tickets; don't know if she even got the check from Dad."

I could hear Morgan taking notes over the phone, her pen scratching the pad quickly trying to keep up.

"And then what happened?"

"Nothing. We waited. Thanksgiving came and passed without another call confirming she'd be coming home for Christmas. Neither Dad nor I said anything. My father believed that she was fine and would be home for Christmas. In the back of our minds, I think we realized she wasn't coming home, but my father held out hope longer than the rest of us. So many thoughts raced through my head. They were too much for my sixteen-year-old mind to process.

"I remember being scared and thinking, how could she just disappear? Why isn't she reaching out to us? Where is she? And I just kept praying, 'Dear God, please keep her safe.'"

"And your mother knew nothing about Marcia coming home at this point?"

"Right. My father didn't want to get her hopes up just to crush them if Marcia was blowing us off. But as Christmas approached and Marcia hadn't called to let us know when she'd be arriving, my Dad got noticeably more worried. A couple of days before Christmas, he and my mom turned in early, and I heard her crying from my bedroom. I knew he told her.

"That Christmas, Mom was a ghost of who she'd been. The pain and anguish on my mother's face said so much without her saying a word. She and Dad spoke in hushed tones a lot of the time, and I knew it was Marcia they were talking about. She continued to cry through that broken-hearted Christmas season while seeing no glimmer of hope in sight."

"That must have been awful, Darlene. I'm so sorry you had to go through that. Did you share the same sentiments with your mom or…?"

"No, I couldn't believe Marcia was gone. I figured something better came up; some friends whisked her off on an epic Christmas vacation or something, and that she'd eventually come home with some lavish apology and make it up to us." I thought about it again, then emphatically concluded, "No, I never thought she was dead."

"So Christmas comes and goes, then what happened? What did your parents do?" Morgan inquired.

"It was after Christmas that my parents decided they needed to contact the Gwinnett County Police Station and file a missing report. Sergeant John Latty was assigned Marcia's case, and he informed my parents that the investigation would start and that they would be in contact for additional information.

"By the end of January, though, I knew she wouldn't be coming home. I locked myself in my room and played music loudly. I hung out with friends. I tried to live life like nothing was wrong. I didn't want to think of Marcia. I tried to swallow the pain and lock it away. But it was next to impossible.

"Every time the phone would ring, I would wonder if it would be the police station. When I was in school, I would wonder if I'd be called down to the high school office informing me that they had information. I continued to function, mimicking a daily routine, which consisted of putting on a 'happy smile' while deep down inside… I was dying."

chapter 8

Morgan mused quietly for a moment, then switched gears. "Okay, can you tell me more about your family's contact in Georgia and how that came about?"

"Yeah. At church, there was a couple, the Reardons, who had a friend living in Georgia. Before Marcia left, we had the couple over for dinner. They arranged with our parents for their friend, George, to check in on Marcia from time to time, make sure she was getting on all right, and report back to Mom and Dad. You know.

"Well, when Marcia didn't come home for Christmas or New Year, my parents had decided not to discuss it with anyone from the church due to the uncertainty at the time. However, they did think it might be beneficial for them to update the Reardons about Marcia's circumstance."

☙

The Reardons approached my parents after church one day in March and asked how Marcia was doing. It was a godsend. Sitting in the front pew, my parents filled them in quickly in hushed tones. I hovered a few rows back, neither wanting to hear their whispers nor wanting to miss out on pertinent information.

"I wonder if George could contact the police station down there and see if he can help in any way," Mr. Reardon volunteered.

My parents quickly agreed to have Mr. Reardon contact George about the situation. After all, George was from that area and could possibly be of additional assistance.

The Reardons were as worried as my parents and hurried home to call their friend, George.

Later that night, our phone rang, and it was the Reardons. George had recalled a black and white sketch of a missing person that was aired on the local television news station in November, 1986. He was going to ask the police if he could see the sketching as he may possibly know who that person was.

My heart sank. I chided myself inwardly to stay strong, but I retreated into my cocoon of anxiety and fear. I wasn't really certain if I wanted to hear the outcome, but I knew I had to hear the results. Escaping reality was my coping skill to be able to function fully.

In the days that followed, George asked my parents for a photo of Marcia, which they mailed immediately, and he took it to the Gwinnett County Police Department. Then Sergeant Latty contacted my parents to get Marcia's dental records released to their department.

I couldn't handle overhearing these conversations. They sent my mind spiraling. What could this mean? Did I even want to know? This could *not* be Marcia. She was alive. She just chose to go away for a while without contacting us. She is fine. She will be back home. My mind tried to tell me anything but what my gut knew.

It was late March, a few weeks after George had visited the Gwinnett County Police Department when the phone rang. The phone barely stood a chance against my father's anxiety. It rang once and was off the hook. There was only silence for a moment before the unbearable wailing began.

The phone call verified that the dental records confirmed that the sketch on the news station in November of 1986 was indeed Marcia. My precious sister, Marcia. How could this happen? What happened to her? How could she be gone at such a young age? My only sister, who I longed to have a relationship with, was gone. I lost it all. I lost that older sibling that I looked up to.

Running to my peach-colored bedroom, I launched myself into my twin-sized bed and cried beneath the 1980s heartthrob posters on my walls.

My parents called our church's youth leader, Diane, whom I was very close to. Diane came over and allowed me to continue to grieve. She sat on my bed and held me while I sobbed. It felt like a nightmare that I could not awaken from, and when I did finally fall asleep that night, I awoke to the anguish of the next day's reality—a life without my sister.

☙

"We learned that Marcia had been killed on November 19, 1986, where she was found by two hunters in the woods. Her body was in a morgue for one month until she was unable to be claimed. A Presbyterian minister had buried her on December 23, 1986, as a *Jane Doe*." The tears spilled over now, and emotion began to clog my throat. Thinking of my sister lying in a cold morgue, alone and unidentified for months, was horribly sickening. I didn't want to remember Marcia that way, cold, alone, empty.

"Despite living on a small income, my parents paid to have her grave exhumed and her body flown home so we could give her a proper burial," I spat out between the tears. "I don't even know where they came up with the kind of money for that sort of thing, but they did. We buried her here in Pennsylvania three days after Easter of 1987." It was a cold April, and I remembered the way the ground crunched under our dress shoes at the graveside. But that day, the sun peeked out, a reminder of God's presence nearby.

"I'm so sorry, Darlene," Morgan winced.

I was careful not to get my hopes up when Morgan first reached out. Now, every time we spoke, it was getting harder and harder to keep my heart open to the possibility of hope.

"You know what's crazy, Morgan? God has continued to show up for us in this storm. When I saw the police sketch, it looked nothing like Marcia, but God used George to help us find her. A few days after we received the call confirming her death, I came home to several roses. My mother informed me that they were from a doctor in Georgia with a note that said, "Not everyone from the Gwinnett County area is evil." What a sweet gesture from a stranger!"

"Then, a few days later, as we dealt with Marcia's belongings, we realized her treasured sewing machine was left in a storage unit along with a few of her other precious belongings. In trying to find a way to get her things, a stranger offered to pack it all up and drive it to Pennsylvania to return it to us. Morgan, that kinda stuff doesn't just happen!"

Morgan was silent. I didn't know how to interpret her stillness, but I was reminded of one other thing to share.

"And lastly, despite the trauma of losing my sister and being unable to remember the date of her funeral, I found a box of my mother's letters detailing the events in chronological order. It was April 22. I hadn't known that for over thirty years. It was 'Easter' to me. God helped me find that answer! Don't you see? I know God is working on this, and he is going to help us find the truth."

"You know I can't make any promises, but I'm going to do everything in my power to find answers for your family."

When we hung up, I closed my eyes and brought my forehead to my knees.

God,
Please help me get through this. The pain of losing my sister was enough the first time. I don't know how much more I can go through. Please send help, heal my heart, and take this pain away.
I don't know how you can use all this for good, but I know your word is true. Please make good on your promise and work this all out for good.
In Jesus' Name,
Amen

And he who searches hearts knows what is the mind of the Spirit, because the Spirit intercedes for the saints according to the will of God.
And we know that for those who love God, all things work together for good, for those who are called according to his purpose.
For those whom he foreknew, he also predestined to be conformed to the image of his Son, in order that he might be the firstborn among many brothers.
Romans 8:27-29

Police identify victim

By Jon McKenna
Gwinnett Daily News

A murder victim who was buried as Jane Doe in a pauper's grave in Lawrenceville last December has been identified through dental records, authorities said Wednesday.

Marcia Jean Burkett, 18, had moved to Atlanta last July after graduating from high school in Philipsburg, Pa., said her father, the Rev. Ned Burkett. She sought a career in fashion design, he said.

After Gwinnett County police sent for dental records from Philipsburg, forensic odontologist Dr. Thomas David of Atlanta Tuesday matched them with molds taken of Miss Burkett's teeth, said Coroner Randy Simpson.

Authorities last month began investigating the possibility that Miss Burkett was the woman found in woods off Shackleford Road on Nov. 19, 1986, according to her father. A family friend saw a police composite sketch on television and contacted authorities because it resembled Miss Burkett, he said.

She had been strangled, raped and beaten, detectives said after the body was discovered by two men crossing the wooded area.

When local efforts to identify the victim failed and the national missing persons computer network turned up nothing, the county paid to bury her as Jane Doe in a Lawrenceville cemetery.

The body will be exhumed for burial in Pennsylvania later this week, Simpson said.

In December, the body of another female murder victim was discovered only about a half-mile from the woods where Miss Burkett was found. She later was identified through fingerprint records in a police criminal file as Dawn Elise Cobben, a transient.

Gwinnett detectives said they have been investigating the possibility that the same person was responsible for the deaths.

The investigation is continuing, but there are no suspects, police spokesman Larry Walton said.

Marcia last contacted her parents in October to say she would be home for Christmas, the Rev. Burkett said Wednesday in a telephone interview from Philipsburg, a town of about 3,500 that is 25 miles west of State College, home of Pennsylvania State University. He is a Methodist minister.

BODY From page 1C

He said the family kept believing Marcia was alive.

She had no relatives or close friends in Atlanta; she basically struck out on her own, Burkett said.

"I didn't want here to go, but I couldn't persuade her to stay," he said.

She enrolled in fashion design courses at the American College for the Applied Arts in Atlanta, Burkett said. But she dropped out after two weeks, for reasons he isn't sure of, he said.

Marcia then found a job as a waitress at a country club, her father said.

She had moved from the Forest Hills Apartments on the Northeast Expressway access road to another complex on Briarwood Road, to another location he didn't know, the Rev. Burkett said.

He described his daughter as "very likable."

MARCIA JEAN BURKETT

A memorial service was held here Wednesday morning for Marcia Jean Burkett, 18, of Gearhartville, near Philipsburg, who was murdered while a student in Gwinnett County, Georgia.

Police in Georgia have said that she was a victim of a homicide in the Atlanta area sometime last year. Her body was found on November 19, 1986, by construction workers and identification was made only recently through dental records. Police admit they have no clues.

Miss Burkett was born February 10, 1968, in Warren, a daughter of Rev. Ned and Ella Mae (Green) Burkett, who survive. The Rev. Burkett is pastor of the Free Methodist Church in Gearhartville.

She was a graduate of the Philipsburg-Osceola Mills High School in 1986 and had gone to Atlanta to attend school.

Surviving, in addition to her parents, are a brother and sister, Dale and Darlene, both at home. Also surviving is a grandmother, Helen Burkett of Gary, NY.

The memorial service was held at the

Body identified as missing Pa. teen

ATLANTA (AP) — Marcia Jean Burkett's parents heard from her last October, and expected her home to Pennsylvania for Christmas. But she was buried in a pauper's grave in Gwinnett County two days before that holiday, the unknown victim of an unknown assailant.

"There's a lot we don't understand, and probably never will, unless they make an arrest," said her father, the Rev. Ned Burkett, from his home in the small community of Gearhartville, Pa., near Phillipsburg.

"This was a country girl, she was not used to city ways, and city people can identify us so quickly," he said of his daughter, who was finally identified last month.

Burkett spoke in an interview with The Atlanta Constitution published in today's editions.

"I'm just terrified of cities, and personally I won't even go into one. If I had had to go down to claim her body, I don't know what I would have done.

"I know that her killer's still loose, and I'm aware of that every day."

Miss Burkett was 18 when she left her home to pursue a career in fashion design by attending the American College for the Applied Arts in Atlanta last summer.

Within two weeks she had quit without notice, and was working as a waitress. She telephoned her parents Oct. 19, sounding in good spirits. She would be home for Christmas, she told them. It was the last time they heard from her.

Her partially clad body was discovered a month later by a pair of hunters in a wooded construction waste site in Gwinnett County. She had been beaten, strangled and raped.

She carried no identification. She was unknown for four months, although a police artist's drawing appeared in newspapers and on television. Her parents' calls to Atlanta and DeKalb County police from late December on were lost in a sea of missing person reports.

Two days before Christmas, she was buried in a plain casket in the pauper's section of Shadow Lawn Cemetery in Lawrenceville.

She was identified after a Loganville couple who had moved to Georgia from central Pennsylvania learned of the Burkett's missing daughter. Her description resembled the drawing of the unknown victim they had seen in the news. The couple took a picture of the missing teenager to Gwinnett police when they returned home.

Authorities identified Marcia Burkett in mid-April from dental records.

chapter 9

Thwack.

A large stack of papers and manila folders dropped on the table on the screen in front of me.

Morgan lived in Tennessee, working as an intern for a private investigator. Between the cases she worked for them, she devoted time to searching for the truth of what happened to Marcia. We had been meeting a lot over Zoom since the pandemic began, but it was usually weeks or months between our points of contact.

"Hey, Darlene, thanks for meeting with me. It's been a little crazy over here, but I wanted to update you on what I've got so far." She reorganized her stack of folders. "I have good news and bad news. Which do you want first?"

I sipped my coffee and noticed my hand trembling ever so slightly. The cup thudded as I placed it back on the desk, knotting my icy fingers together in my lap.

"Bad news," I decided.

"Okay, bad news first: I submitted another request for Marcia's entire case file. I was very specific about everything I needed to try to prevent them from denying it. I asked for the autopsy report, notes, pictures, videos, interviews, interview reports, statements, death certificate, coroner's report, crime scene photos and reports, evidence logs, 911 calls, and DNA.

"But I was denied with the statute: *O.C.G.A. § 50-18-72(a)(4)-Records of law enforcement, prosecution, or regulatory agencies in any pending investigation or prosecution of criminal or unlawful activity, other than initial police arrest reports and initial incident reports.*"

My chest deflated as the air knocked out of me.

"Again?"

She nodded, biting her lip.

It had been two years since Morgan's first message arrived in my inbox and four years since she began her investigation into Marcia's disappearance and death on her own. It seemed every time we made one step forward, the criminal justice system shuttered us back three steps. Every petition and request for information Morgan made had gone either unopened, unanswered, or denied.

"And the good news?"

I picked at my nails as she shuffled the papers, looking for what she wanted to tell me about. A small plaque on my desk reminded me that *God works all things together for good*. My dear friend Marla gifted it to me a year ago when she began helping me through this process. Silently, I thanked God for her and the hard but worthy journey of healing she was helping me through.

"Okay, here it is," Morgan said through the screen, holding up a folder. "I had a call with Sergeant John Richter at the Gwinnett County Police Department." She paused, looking up at me before continuing. "He informed me that this is still an active case, and that is why nothing can be released to me. He stated that there is currently newfound DNA testing being done, but it could take up to six months to get the results."

Newfound DNA? I couldn't explain the throbbing in my head, the way my pulse raced as warm panic flooded my body. *Wasn't this good news?* This *was* good news.

I opened my mouth to speak, but nothing came out.

"Darlene, did you hear me? Are you still there?"

I nodded, my mouth parched.

"Do you know what this means?" Her eyes were wide, and a slow smile spread across her face. "It means that we might actually catch whoever did this. There is an active person of interest. This is huge!"

She was right. It was a big deal—an active person of interest? The police had never had a real suspect, not really. When Marcia's body was found, there seemed to be so little evidence they couldn't even identify her. But now there was a person of interest? I knew in my mind I should be elated. Justice was finally coming through over thirty years later. But instead, all I could see was a man, evil incarnate, hurting my sister and walking away scotch-free for thirty years.

This boogeyman haunted my nightmares for years. I felt out of control, unable to do anything about this man walking around the earth just out of reach for the punishment he deserved. It scared me. Irrationally, I worried he would come after me next. Ludicrous, I know. But this reminder, an active person of interest, revived the boogeyman I fought so hard to hold at bay. He was real, and we were hopefully closing in. Would the police catch him this time?

"Did they say how they came across this suspect?" I tried to keep the shiver out of my voice.

"Shortly after Marcia's body was found, there was another female also found murdered in very close proximity. This female's name was Dawn Cobeen. Sergeant Richter believes that Marcia and Dawn's murders are related and done by the same individual."

"Another murder?" My heart thrummed. This was more than I could handle. An irrational flood of jealousy hit me. I didn't want Morgan to look into *someone else's* death; I wanted her focused on Marcia's death. I breathed through the intrusive thoughts and closed my eyes to pray a quick prayer: *Give me strength, God. Hold the thoughts at bay.*

"We don't know anything for sure right now," Morgan responded, and I opened my eyes to watch her scan the report in her hands, "but it could be a lead. If this guy has hurt other women, there's a chance he left behind some evidence. I'm going to look into Miss Cobeen's case and see what I can find."

"All right, thanks for everything you're doing."

"Of course, Darlene. There is absolutely no reason that this should have happened to Marcia, and there is no reason that this case should have gone cold. Discovering the truth will be extremely traumatic, but it will provide answers and, eventually, a sense of peace."

chapter 10

Morgan was right—reliving the trauma of losing Marcia had been taking a toll on me. That night, I tossed and turned. Every time I closed my eyes, I thought of Marcia's lifeless body and the evil man who hurt her.

Throwing back the covers, I tip-toed from the room, careful not to wake Matt. I needed to see Marcia.

The family album rested on a bookshelf in the den. I grabbed it, grabbed a blanket from the living room, and curled up on the leather chair. Flipping through Mom and Dad's wedding photos and Dale's baby photos, I stopped when I reached 1968. The year Marcia was born. I ran my fingers over the images one at a time. Her crystal blue eyes shone through the old film photographs perfectly. I spent an hour pouring over her pictures and stopped when I reached a photo from our last family home in Philipsburg. It was the last time we were all together before Marcia moved out.

In the photo, she and I are lying out in the yard in the summer sun. She squinted at the camera in annoyance, and I beamed, throwing my hair over my shoulder. I hold the album to my heart and lean my head back as I relive a good memory.

☙

The year was 1983, and I was finishing my usual Saturday morning routine watching Don Cornelius wrap up *Soul Train* as the dancers came out for one final dance down the aisle. Summertime was beginning to peak in Philipsburg. We had just moved to the area, and the only thing I found enjoyable was lying out in the sun until I made some new friends.

"Marcia!" I called from outside her bedroom door. "Let's go outside and get some sun. It's nice out."

Marcia opened the door and looked me up and down. "Fine, but *I'm* taking the good lounge chair." There was only one good lounge chair if you could even call it that.

Marcia changed and met me outside on the lawn, where I cast a beach towel down on the grass next to the boombox. Marcia took the chair; it was bright yellow vinyl with adjustable arms. Both ends folded into the middle, but with one wrong turn, you'd be a goner trapped in the middle of the chair.

I didn't fight Marcia on it. I knew it was only a matter of time until her fair skin burnt, and she'd run inside, leaving me the chair to finish basking in.

It was the perfect summer day. Marcia settled into the chair, smearing baby oil on her arms and legs while I cranked up the boombox. It was my new *Whitney Houston Greatest Hits* cassette tape. She was such a hit! I loved her song "Greatest Love of All" and tapped my feet to the song.

After about an hour of rotating in the sun, the lobster look on her face revealed it all: Marcia was burnt and annoyed. She stomped inside like I knew she would, and I snagged her chair so I could finish my tan. I was desperately hoping Dale would take us to the rink; my golden tan would glow with my fluorescent green shirt under the cool arcade lights.

Two hours later, I went inside to wash off. I just had to convince Dale to make the forty-five minute trip from Philipsburg to Bellefonte's Skateland. Dale was eighteen and had a jet-black Camaro. It was so much cooler showing up to the skating rink in his ride than in our family station wagon.

He hesitated and gave us a difficult time at first, but with the two of us coaxing him, he finally agreed.

Mom overheard and threw her two cents in. "You two have to be home by eleven o'clock."

Marcia and I ran to get ready. I worked on curling my hair and dousing it in half a can of Aquanet. I craved the high-hair look that all the girls had; I knew that only Aquanet could keep it up all night.

"Hurry up," Dale yelled. "I'm leaving now!"

Marcia bustled out of her room with a record in hand. She had the newest hit of Bonnie Tyler, "Total Eclipse of the Heart," and she was convinced that Skateland didn't have the record yet. We quickly grabbed our shoes and hopped into Dale's car.

The two-door Camaro meant I had to crawl in the back. The air inside was stifling from the day's heat, and I worried my makeup would melt. But as they rolled the windows down and cruised down the street toward Bellefonte, I worried for my hair.

"Please don't roll the windows too far," I pleaded. This hair could endure a night of skating but might not endure the fifty-five-mile-an-hour wind. They grumbled and obliged.

Dale dropped us off at seven p.m., reminding us that he would be back to pick us up at eleven p.m. *Sharp.*

Inside, the rink was masterfully designed, with lights all around the inner rink and the arcade along the outer edge. The snack bar was directly ahead when you entered the building, and there were booths along the wall where you could watch others skate. Along the right side of the entrance, past the skate rental, was the DJ area with double-wide glass windows where you could see who was the host for the evening.

We knew the owners of the rink, and they would randomly allow Dale and Marcia to help out with DJing the music. Marcia was all amped up in anticipation that they'd let her play her new record.

Past the DJ area was an entire wall of the arcade arena ranging from games like *Donkey Kong, Galaga, Frogger, Pac-Man,* and *Asteroids.* For me, *Ms. Pac-Man* was the best of all games. A quarter went a long way, especially if you were able to master the game.

Marcia stopped to put on the skates she had brought: white roller skates with big yellow pom-poms on the front. They were so popular. I couldn't get my own skates yet due to my feet still growing. Oh, how I loved hers and admired the things she had, but I always had to wait to enjoy those things it seemed.

I hurried to the skate rental and saw my friends, Kerri and Julie, in line already! I usually only saw them once a month when our youth group got together with other churches, but I knew they'd be here tonight. I had so much to talk to them about and was also looking around for a cute boy to skate with.

"Funky Town" was playing when we skated to the floor, and the rink began to fill. I noticed Marcia was talking to the owners' boys, Kevin and Keith. I figured she was gearing up for her song.

We skated for about an hour when they announced the next song would be couple skating. There was no one I anticipated to skate with so I headed over to the snack bar to grab a pretzel and soda. Kerri, Julie, and I continued catching up about the past month's activities.

The first song started to play, "On the Wings of Love" by Jeffrey Osborne. *Man, what a beautiful song!*

Marcia stood behind the glass area where the DJ diligently prepared the next selection of music. Her song was up next. *She's so lucky,* I thought. As the piano slowly faded out, Bonnie Tyler started to belt out her brand-new song.

Marcia was glowing about this opportunity. She stayed in the DJ area for several songs before she came out to finish skating with us.

Time quickly evaded us, and I knew it was almost time to go. Dale would be restless if we weren't outside waiting for him when he got here. My feet were hurting, and I was tired from the day's activities, not to mention that the sun had zapped me out.

When we got home, I tried to stay awake for some of the *Night Tracks* before it was over. Marcia and I were able to watch the top three from the ten countdown before it ended. I was out for the night, completely exhausted.

The next morning came early. As a preacher's kids, we had an early morning church to attend. Marcia headed down to church early the next morning since she was playing the piano for that morning's worship service.

After eight years of learning piano from our next-door neighbor, Kathy, when we lived in Fleming, Marcia had really mastered the talent.

I managed to drag myself out of bed, so I was there before my father stared me down from the pulpit. I walked in just as Marcia was beginning the first song of the service, "How Great Thou Art." The church was filling in, and I snuck into my usual spot in the pew. The church windows were already opened wide for the morning sermon.

I sat through the sermon, thinking about our Sunday lunch, knowing that Mom was making my favorite: twice-baked potatoes and grilled chicken.

When church ended, Marcia and I walked the block up the street to home and quickly changed our clothes while listening to Casey Kasem's countdown from one hundred.

Sundays were such a relaxing day out of the week. We never really did much on those days, just hung around the house. I had no new friends so Marcia and I would mostly do things together when she felt like hanging out with her younger sister.

☙

"Dar?"

I awoke to someone shaking my shoulder.

"Rabbi, I think you fell asleep out here," Matt said. The use of his nickname for me always warmed my heart.

I looked around. Spread around me on the couch and floor were pictures of Marcia, Dale, and me as kids. I squinted as the sun filtered through the blinds. It was morning. I realized for the first time in a long time I fell asleep thinking of Marcia without having nightmares.

chapter 11

"Hunter and I are leaving for Atlanta tomorrow. I'll see what I can find out. I'll keep you posted!" My phone pinged with a new message from Morgan.

I must have read that blue text bubble a hundred times but still couldn't piece together a response. Hunter was Morgan's fiance. I thought back to the engagement photos she posted on Facebook. The sweet girl deserved some love after the difficulties she'd faced. I closed out of the Facebook Messenger app and slid the phone across the desk, *away from me*.

I went to work early that day to try to get my mind off the trip, but the anxiety only followed me there. Morgan had insisted on going to Atlanta from the beginning, something I never could have fathomed doing. Now, I was beginning to worry for her. Could she really find the guy that did this? Would the police there even talk to her? *Was it a complete waste of time?*

A knock on my door broke my thoughts, and I looked up to see the newest nurse in training, Susan, poking her head through the frame. She was our youngest nurse, having graduated from a training high school as a CNA. Her blue scrubs made her large eyes pop in a dazzling, scary way. It reminded me of Marcia, and my eyes slid to the photo of her and me on my desk.

In the photo, our mother had us dressed in matching gingham dresses and saddle shoes for church. Marcia was eight, and I was six; those were the years Marcia sported a boyish bowl cut that she never forgave our mother for.

"Mrs. Gildersleeve, Miss Jordan asked me to come and let you know that the group's ready for you in the rec room." She lingered in the doorway, her eyes on me and her head cocked to the side like a puppy. "Is everything all right, Mrs. Gildersleeve?"

"Fine. Thank you, Susan; I'll be there in a moment." I stood from my desk, not returning her eye contact. My eyes were still glued on Marcia's photo, her dour expression glowering up at me.

Susan took a brazen step forward into my office, her eyes dancing around my desk, landing on the photo of Marcia and me. When she saw it, she noticeably brightened. "Awe, is that your sister?" She reached for the photo, but I beat her to it, tipping it forward so the photo was against the desk.

I cleared my throat.

Susan looked injured—the horror at her social no-no and fear of punishment were painted across her cheeks.

"What happened?" she whispered, nodding to the frame now lying face down between us.

I stepped around the desk and breezed past her, throwing open the door.

"She died. Car accident," I said over my shoulder, then I left her in the office.

My heels clacked on the tiled linoleum as I made my way down the corridors to the rec room. My heart thudded from the lie, but I didn't care. It angered me so much when people would ask about Marcia. They all acted like they had a right to know what happened to her.

But I had learned the hard way, one too many times, what happened when I told people the truth.

I suppose it was my fault. I assumed that all people shared a sense of human decency. But as I grew older and I shared the truth about Marcia, the questions only got more shameless. People heard the word *murder* and wanted to know how it happened, who did it, did he assault her first, was it quick?

Angry tears pricked in my eyes, and I swerved right to stop in the bathroom before leading group therapy for the day.

༺༻

The day after we got the call of Marcia's death, our house was eerily quiet. The only sounds were the passing activity of cars and folks outside. Around noon, the familiar thwack of paper on the pavement meant that the newspaper was there.

My mother went to retrieve it from the stoop, but her gasp had both Dad and me running to see what it was.

I crooned over her shoulder to see the paper she was holding. There, alongside the front page news article, was the headline "Police Identify Victim." It had only been a day, and the local newspaper already ran her story. I gasped in shock, too.

My mother and father silently read the article to themselves, and I saw the sun glisten in the quiet tears that ran down her cheek. I peered around her arm to read, too.

Details I hadn't known about Marcia's death were printed in black and white for everyone to read, speculating how she died and describing what happened to her body in excruciating detail. It was too much.

I ran to my room and locked the door.

The next day, I decided to put the newspaper article behind me. I couldn't handle all the emotions it drudged up and didn't want to. So I went to my friend Rhonda's house, determined to find normalcy wherever I could.

When I arrived at Rhonda's house, her mom let me in. I found Rhonda standing in the living room, kicking something under the couch.

What was she trying to hide from me? Why does she look so frightened?

I peered down under the couch, against her protests, and grabbed at what she was trying to hide.

A newspaper.

To my surprise, there was another article about Marcia in our local newspaper. I read and reread the words printed until they blurred in a teary mess. More details about Marcia's disappearance and death that I hadn't known were there. A hot rush of sickness coursed through me. The idea that my sister was being permanently remembered in this disgusting manner was unacceptable. I was embarrassed and angry. I couldn't stand for it.

"Are you kidding me?!" I yelled. "That's it, I'm contacting *The Progress*. I've had enough."

We were trying to navigate through completely unchartered waters, and the stupid newspapers continued to profit off our pain. For what?

"This isn't entertainment!" I said, jabbing the paper with my finger. "This is people's lives; parading their suffering and trauma was as dehumanizing as it got!"

I had no idea what I was doing, but before I knew it, I was walking home and calling the newspaper office to speak to the editor. Steam was rolling off me in angry crimson waves.

When the editor answered, I gave him a piece of my mind. "If one more article is published, the newspaper will be hearing from our lawyer!"

The editor quickly apologized, and there were no more articles published from that day on.

To clear my head, I went for a bike ride around the block, and later that afternoon, I came home to several roses on our dining room table.

"Who sent these red roses?" I asked Mom.

"I have no idea who they're from, but the note said, 'Not everyone from Gwinnett County is evil. A doctor in Georgia.'"

That stopped me in my tracks. It wasn't until that moment that I realized I had actually begun to believe that very sentiment. Although in my mind, it stretched further than Georgia, right into our backyard.

"Wow, what a sweet gesture from a stranger," I thought to myself.

⁂

Looking in the mirror, I blotted my eyes carefully to avoid smearing my makeup and took a deep breath. The topic for group therapy today was repressed emotions. I couldn't feel any more like an imposter at this moment if I tried. I needed to let go of this. I had been reading verses about forgiveness lately. While I wasn't ready to forgive the man who did this, I could forgive Susan for being uncouth and nosy. I could forgive the newspaper and editor for doing their jobs, albeit crassly.

I closed my eyes in the silent bathroom and prayed for forgiveness. I prayed for help to forgive Susan and all the others before her who pestered me with the immodest questions about Marcia. I prayed for the strength to blot out the memories the newspaper bore into me and waited on the Lord for his deliverance as the sink tap dripped slowly. My heart calmed until it nearly matched the leak—drip, drip, drip. The anger whooshed out of me like a hot air balloon popping—deflated, but it was a relief. I was no longer simmering and ready to pop.

 I thanked God, threw away the crumpled paper towel, and headed out to the rec room.

chapter 12

The metal chairs squeaked and screamed against the freshly waxed floor. The group was small today. I looked around our inpatient crew for the day: two women, one seemingly old enough to be my mother and one young enough to be my daughter. The young girl's face was hollow, her eyes vacant. Her clothes hung loosely on her bone-thin frame.

The two men joining us were both older. One grumbled in an overmedicated stupor while the other fidgeted restlessly. His eyes darted around the room. On one wall, we had a piano, and on the other, a locked cabinet with our art supplies. Hanging on the cabinet was a sign that read, "I can and will be strong again."

I let that sentiment fill my heart and mind for a moment as I waited for everyone to settle in. A nurse and orderly joined us in the room, hovering in the background before we began.

"Today's session is on grief. We're going to talk about the stages of grief and the importance of processing our emotions." I shifted in my seat and looked around the group. Their eyes were anywhere but on me. The frail young woman picked at her cuticles until one bled, and she shoved it in her mouth.

"Can anyone tell me the first stage of grief?" I asked, looking from the small older woman to the fidgeting man sitting next to her. They both politely smiled and looked away.

"The first stage of grief is denial." I held up the printout I made the day before. Under the word was a picture of a girl with her hands over her ears. "Can anyone describe what denial is?"

"It's a river in Africa," barked the fidgeter with a laugh.

"Ha, you're not wrong. Denial in terms of grief is when we avoid the truth of our situation. Have any of you struggled with denial in your own life?"

Again, I was met with silence save for the voice in my head. I couldn't help but think of my sister and the process of grief our family endured. I could have been the Queen of Denial.

"Let's continue. The second stage of grief is anger." I held up another printout depicting anger. The picture was of a man yelling skyward with clenched fists. Somewhere in my chest, I felt a pang. I tried not to be angry with God when we lost Marcia, but some days, it was hard to control my emotions.

"I know that emotion well…" the older woman said with a sigh, crossing her arms. "The good Lord gives, and the good Lord takes away." She gave a little harrumph as though finalizing her point.

I blinked at her, stunned for a moment longer than I'd like to admit. Had she read my mind? Or was the emotion so clearly displayed on my face?

"God? HA!" The fidgeter let out a coarse laugh. "What's he got to do with any of this? If he were real, bad things wouldn't happen."

"You both bring up some interesting points," I interjected before the discussion could get carried away. "Anger can be a difficult emotion to process. It's normal when we experience pain or loss to try to rationalize our suffering. We will either blame someone or 'God'—whatever we believe in—or we'll turn inwards and shame ourselves. While it's important to feel all the emotions associated with grief, it's equally as important not to get stuck in any stage. At some point, we must be willing to release the emotions and their hold on us."

As I said those words, a wave of understanding ran over me. I was no longer sitting in the rec room, huddled up in a group therapy circle; I was sitting in the college counselor's office during my freshman year.

☙

The first thing I noticed in the counselor's office was the fake green plant in the corner of the room. It was covered in dust and reminded me of the mask I had been wearing for a year and a half.

It had been almost two years since I'd seen Marcia's face. She was never truly gone to me since I hadn't seen her body. I understood why Father insisted on a closed casket, but something ate at me inside. None of us had seen her. Not really. How could we be sure she was gone?

I thought of Marcia's beautiful blue eyes—*No, stop it, Darlene.* I shook my head just a smidge to push back the image and the tears threatening to spill over. Marcia had to be gone; she wouldn't abandon us like this. I couldn't decide which reality was worse, a world where Marcia was still out there ignoring us or one where she no longer existed.

My heart raced at the intrusive thoughts, and I immediately hated them. The thoughts that plagued me. I couldn't control them, and it was driving me crazy. My fingers twitched in hunger. I needed to control something. Anything.

I found a loose thread on the hem of my shirt that had been growing baggier and baggier over the weeks, and I yanked it.

Across from me, a woman in a beige suit with boxy shoulder pads sat shuffling papers. I picked at my cuticles as the thoughts swirled in my head. I didn't want to be here. I couldn't be here.

I sighed, already resigning myself to be tight-lipped so I could get out of here as fast as possible.

"So, Miss Burkett, why don't you tell me about what brings you in today?" She slid her round wire frames up her nose and looked me over, pen hovering over the pad in her lap.

Was she going to make me say it? My jaw almost hung open at the thought of her audacity. I was sure it was in her notes. They made me fill out paperwork for this appointment that my roommate forced me to take.

I was quiet for a long moment, debating whether or not to stand up and march out of the room.

"I guess I've been having some…trouble lately." I couldn't help the sardonic tone that eked out.

She looked over the folder that contained all the papers she was reviewing earlier. "It says here that you recently lost your sister? Is that correct?"

I nodded without looking up. She let another large span of silence fall between us until she realized I wouldn't be volunteering any information.

"And I have a note here from your roommate Lisa saying that she was worried about how it was affecting your health."

The sigh that escaped my nostrils was hot, the steam from a volcano before it erupts.

"Why don't you tell me more about your experience with grief, Darlene?"

"Why? So you can pity me?" I bit back at her.

Her eyes softened, and she shifted uncomfortably in her seat. "No, Darlene. I would like to help you if you'll let me."

"I don't need help. And I especially don't need your pity." *What I need is to get this under control.* I almost added that last part, but it died on my tongue.

"Darlene, let's cut to the chase." She took off her glasses and leaned forward. "You've experienced a traumatic event at a young age. You are still in shock. Looking at your report, I estimate you are still in the early stages of grief. Denial, anger… bargaining even? It's okay to struggle with your loss, but what's not okay is to hurt yourself in the process."

She sat back and watched me for a moment before continuing. Her gaze raked over my thinning frame.

"You are lucky to have a roommate who cares enough about you to intervene on your behalf. Now, I can't make you do anything. I can't make you talk to me. But I want you to know that I am here to help you. My door is open to you, and I strongly recommend you take me up on that offer before these unhealthy coping skills make you any sicker."

chapter 13

The group's bickering brought me back to the moment. I wish I could say I listened to the counselor during those first sessions, got myself some help, and worked through my issues in that moment, but I didn't. The memory of my early days in group therapy gave me a heart full of compassion for the four in front of me now.

"Okay, I hear you all," I spoke over them to cut off their squabbling. "This is a very sensitive topic for all of you to discuss. Why don't we put a pin in it here and come back to it later? I have another set of questions I'd like to present to today's group for discussion."

Each of the four slowly settled and turned away from each other, back towards me.

"Let's talk about coping skills. What are some unhealthy coping skills we use in our grief?"

"Drinking."

"Smoking."

"Drugs."

"Men."

They were quick to volunteer information about unhealthy coping skills.

"Not eating."

My eyes shot to the young girl. She reminded me so much of my daughter, the same honey-blonde hair and blue eyes, the picture of youthfulness. Except the girl in front of me was wasting away slowly. Her diagnosis, her mental illness, was a death sentence if she didn't make a decision to turn it around. My heart broke for her, and I began to understand how God's heart broke for me when I was in her position.

"Unhealthy coping skills rob us of the opportunity to process our suffering and heal. They delay the inevitable and keep us trapped in a limiting mindset.

"How about some healthy coping skills? What are some good ways to process loss?"

The group was quiet. I could practically hear their gears turning, and my heart softened, realizing they couldn't think of any.

"How about calling a friend? So you aren't alone." I watched them as they thought about it, and a couple nodded. "What else?"

"I like to color when I get anxious." The young girl said it like a question, but I smiled at her encouragingly.

"That's a great tool to manage stress and anxiety!"

"I guess I like to bake," The older woman added.

"That's good! Do you like to bake when you're struggling or just any time it suits?"

"Mostly anytime, but it's especially calming when I've had a bad day. Plus, you get to lick the bowl clean, and that always makes me feel better." Her laugh was deep and scratchy like she'd smoked her whole life. Even though it was a shock to my ears, it was a good sound.

It was the sound of hope.

༄

Cleaning up from dinner the next night, my phone pinged with a message from Morgan.

"The Gwinnett County PD won't see me."

I let out an aggravated sigh. After my week at work, I had almost forgotten Morgan was in Georgia trying to meet with the detective on Marcia's case. Of course, they wouldn't; this whole trip was a waste. I was irrationally angry at Morgan. She shouldn't have done this.

A bubble with three dots appeared.

But I typed out a message quicker.

"What do you mean they won't see you?!"

Waiting for her message, I leaned my hip against the counter. Half of the lasagna was left in the pan on the stove, while the other half was in the Tupperware containers littering the granite. I stared at her gray dots, willing her to write back that it was just a joke or some kind of misunderstanding. After having a lovely dinner with my family that completely took my mind off of this struggle, I was thrown right back into my anger and panic.

"They said that because this is an active case, they can't give me any information. But don't worry, Darlene, I'm not that easily dissuaded. Hunter and I are going to make a weekend out of it. See if I can find anything else. I'll keep you posted."

I rinsed my hands off at the sink, giving myself a minute to think.

"What about that other case you mentioned? Is it still an active case, too?" A small flutter of hope stole my breath.

"It's an avenue I'm looking into, but try to manage your expectations."

Well, there went that small figment of hope. Immediately, I felt heavy and exhausted. I just wanted to crawl in bed.

"I'll be praying for you guys." I typed back and locked my phone, leaving it on the counter as I finished putting dinner away.

An hour later, I was in bed, tossing and turning. The restlessness began to feel visceral. I attempted to will my emotions away, hoping they would evaporate, but they persisted. I knew there was only one thing I could do.

I flipped the covers back and swung my legs over the bed. Getting down on my knees, I lay my face on the bed and cried out to God.

God,

This feels impossible! This is awful and painful, and I can't handle it. Honestly, God, I don't know how much more of this I can take. I thought I could do it — reopening Marcia's case and seeking justice — but it's just tearing me apart. You're tearing me apart. Why would you lead me down this road only to give us dead ends? I don't understand. I thought you were a just God, a loving God. But I need you, and you're not showing up for me. Where are you? Can you even hear me?

I sobbed for a while, letting all the frustration pour out. It hurt to cry so much that my eyes began swelling, and my breaths became ragged. But somewhere deep inside, I knew that God was listening. I knew that he was with me.

God,

I'm sorry. This hurts so much, and there's so much I don't understand. Please help me. I know there has to be a better way to deal with this. I'm supposed to be a therapist, someone who helps others heal, and yet I feel so broken. I don't even feel worthy of being helped right now, let alone helping others. I need your healing touch, God. I don't care how you do it, but please heal this grief. Send someone or something my way to change this.

Please, God, I'm desperate.

chapter 14

A month later, Morgan messaged me, asking to call me. It had been torturous waiting for her update on the trip to Georgia. I replied within minutes, and we set up a time to talk the next day.

When my phone buzzed again, I thought it was Morgan, but it was a call from my dear friend, Marla.

"Hello?"

"Hey, Darlene! How are you doing?" Marla's sincere voice was refreshing after the stressful week of work and waiting.

"I'm okay, you know. How are you doing?"

"I'm doing so well, thank you for asking. Do you remember me telling you about that conference I went to a few months ago in Ohio?"

Marla and I have grown close in recent years since we attended the same church. She has been getting more involved in serving, and it is inspiring to see. The woman never quits! Sometimes, I wonder how she finds time to sleep.

"Yeah, I think so. It was about healing or something?"

"Yes! I can't believe you remember!" I could hear her smiling. There was something sweet about her friendship—I had never felt truly appreciated by another friend until I met her. "I was reading my Bible this morning, and I felt like God put you on my heart. I just wanted to check in. It's been a while since we've gotten coffee together. Are you free this week?"

"Yes!"

We made plans and finished our call. As I sat looking forward to this week—a feeling I hadn't had in a while—it dawned on me that Marla never shared the relevance of her trip to Ohio. Granted, I didn't know much about it, but it struck me as strange that we dropped the topic so quickly. I made a mental note to ask her more about it when we had coffee.

❧

"Okay, so the trip wasn't entirely a bust." Morgan's face appeared on my computer screen for a moment before she turned in her seat and reached for her files. It looked like she was calling from her office.

When Morgan first reached out, she had just been a brilliant girl interested in helping a family find answers in tragedy. Now, she worked for a private investigator's company and was licensed to do this work. That small fact gave me more hope than I should trifle with.

"So the Gwinnett County police wouldn't speak with me. They gave me the same run around they'd been giving me over email. But! I did track down some information on the other woman's case, Dawn Cobeen. And before you get your hopes up, it was helpful but not a solid lead."

I appreciated her warning. "Okay, tell me more."

"When we left the PD, I searched Facebook for Dawn's family. I found her brother first, Mark Cobeen. He said he wanted to help but didn't know anything about her case. So he connected me to their sister, Tina." Morgan looked up into the screen at me for a moment. "Darlene, listen to this. Tina said the rumor she heard was that Dawn was going to testify against a drug dealer, and the police think that's probably who killed her, but we really don't know anything. The guy she lived with died shortly after her. If it wasn't the drug dealer who did it, maybe it was the Green River Killer."

My head was spinning. This was a lot of new information. I don't know what I thought had happened to my sister, but neither of these options were listed as possibilities in my mind. Drug dealer? No way. My sister didn't do drugs. She never had a problem before she left, and nothing was found in her toxicology report. It didn't add up.

"Darlene..." Morgan's tone softened, and her brown eyes were sad when they looked at mine. "This was just hearsay from a relative. I know Marcia didn't have a problem, but maybe she saw something she shouldn't have and... Who knows."

I hadn't realized I had said what I had been thinking out loud until then. I looked away, embarrassed.

Morgan shuffled her notes and added, "I ended up requesting Dawn Cobeen's entire case file, but I was told that there were no records with that name."

"Wow, again?" I really started to lose faith in our criminal justice system.

"I know this can be frustrating, hang in there. So, after that request was denied, I revised it. I looked for the incident report for her death and got it."

"So what? Did they just lie? How can they do that? I thought they were supposed to be the good guys?"

"It's not as clear cut as that. Criminal proceedings can be very complicated, and while I'm not justifying what they did, they do try to protect victims' identities. So..." She trailed off, and I just shook my head. I don't know how she constantly puts up with this.

"That's not all. Dawn's sister reached back out and sent me another message. She said: 'Sadly, the police treated my sister's case like she was just a piece of shit and didn't deserve anything, so my parents stopped trying after a few years of figuring out what went wrong. They never gave us any information. We don't have DNA, we have no suspects, we have nothing. We only had a conversation with the guy she lived with. Then he was murdered. My sister was a human being that deserved an explanation. They gave us nothing.'"

Hearing Morgan read the message broke my heart. I understood exactly how Dawn's sister felt. The emotion clouded my mind; I felt myself getting pulled back into the memories and the pain of loss. I couldn't remember what else Morgan had said, so I just shook my head.

"That's awful. It makes me so angry that more isn't being done."

"I know. But did you catch what Tina said about the guy she lived with? He died shortly after Dawn was murdered. So did Marcia's roommate. I think they both saw something they shouldn't have, and someone was tying up loose ends."

Morgan's features were sharp now. She was determined to catch whoever did this. It scared me in a way I couldn't explain. Yes, I was torn up about losing my sister and craving justice, but the idea that someone out there was getting away with multiple murders? It terrified me. What if Morgan got too close and something happened to her? What if this man found out we and the Cobeen family were talking? What if we were next?

"Morgan…" I hesitated, finding the right words to ask my next question. "Are you sure this is safe? I mean, what you're talking about isn't just a one-time sicko. This is a serial killer you're talking about. Aren't you scared?"

Recognition dawned in her eyes, and she set the papers down on her desk. She folded her hands together and leaned into the camera.

"No, I am not, and let me tell you why. I want the perpetrator of this heinous crime to be held accountable for their despicable actions. I want this individual off the streets and in prison where he belongs. It sickens me that this individual could be walking on the streets right now, never suffering any consequences of his horrible actions. This creates the idea in others' heads that they can get away with this with no consequences, and this is a terrible message to spread. People need to know that whether it be six months or sixty years, the investigation will never stop."

Her passionate confession sparked so much emotion in me that I began crying. There was so much relief in knowing I wasn't the only one who cared, the only one trying to find answers. When the police wouldn't help, I felt so isolated and alone, but hearing Morgan's vigor for the case renewed in me a steadfastness to go on. If she wouldn't stop, neither would I.

I brushed the tears out of my eyes. "Thanks, Morgan. I can't really even begin to find words to express my gratitude for all you are doing."

"Marcia suffered and she struggled. She deserves justice. I will not stop until I get answers for what happened to her." Morgan's gaze met mine, and I could see their intensity. It dried up my tears and gave me strength.

"Thank you, Morgan," I whispered, closing my eyes, comforted by her resolve.

She sat back in her chair and shifted her demeanor to her former professionalism. "I have one more thing I want to show you." She held up her phone screen to the webcam. It was blurry for a moment, but then it came into view. In a shaded area, at the base of a tree was a cross with Marcia's name on it.

"We found the location." I heard what she wasn't saying, where Marcia's body had been found, where she had been killed. "Marcia will be remembered." She turned the phone away then, and I tried to remember it, but its details already began fading from memory.

"Can you send that to me?"

"Of course. We bought a wooden cross, painted it, and put it in the ground, where Marcia's body was found. Now, this address is an apartment complex/hotel off of a main road, but I wanted the people that lived there to know that an innocent soul died there."

My heart ached. Marcia will be remembered.

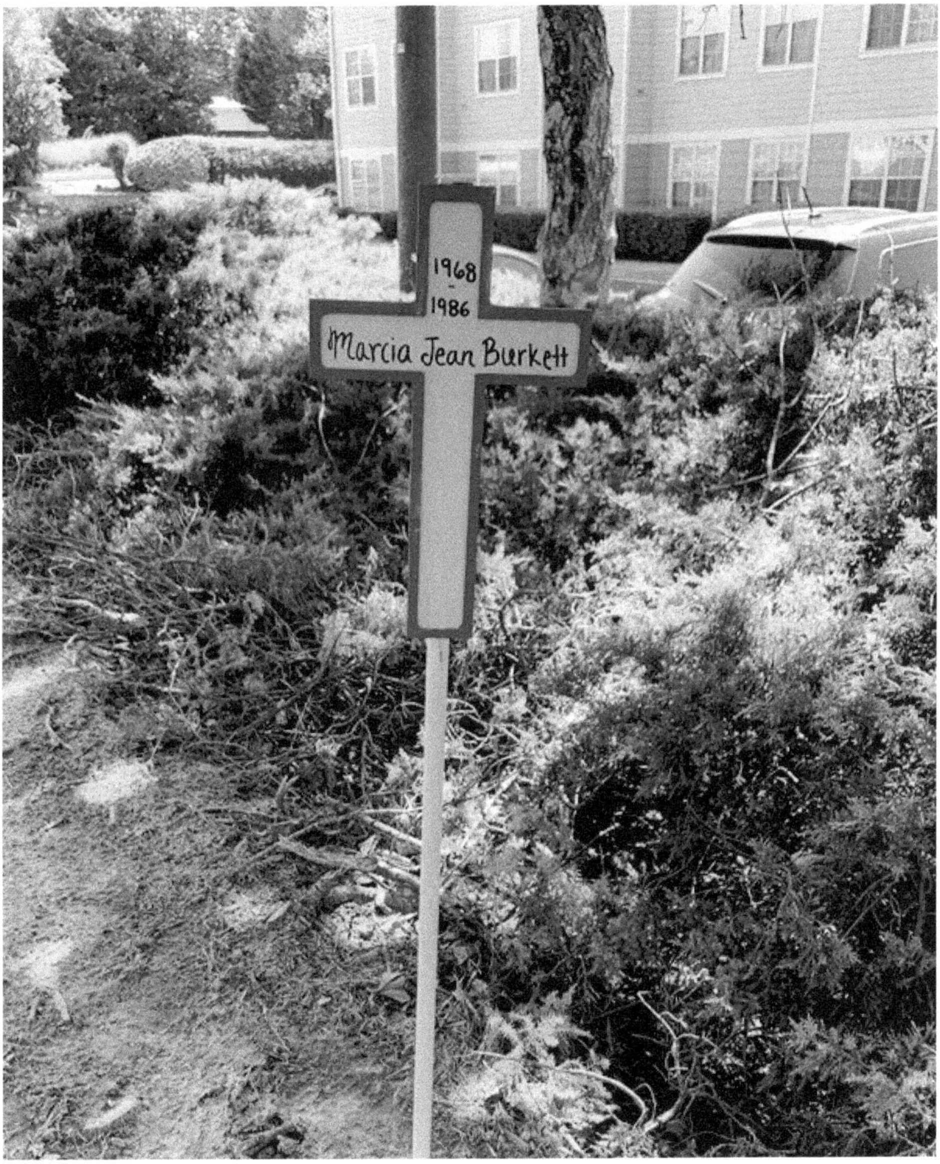
1968
-
1986
Marcia Jean Burkett

chapter 15

It had been four days since Marla called, and I was tidying up the house in anticipation for her arrival. Marla was my friend for many years, and before that, she was my boss.

I was a fresh-faced kid out of college, and Marla gave me my first job working at a group home. With my degree in psychology, I was eager to help those struggling with mental health. I was ready to jump in and serve the organization that Marla was a part of. Looking back makes me realize how naive I was in those early days.

I'd never had a patient lie to me before, mock me, or make up symptoms for prescriptions, and I never believed they would. Fluffing the pillows on the couch, I shook my head at the memory of a girl who did just that. There are so many things I know now that I wish I could tell her.

Ding dong.

The doorbell rang, and I trotted to the door to find Marla; her sweet, petite frame barreled towards me to embrace me. She smelled like patchouli and sunshine and hugged like it was the end of the world. I adored my friend.

"Come in! I have coffee brewing." I opened the door wider for her to step through.

As we ambled to the kitchen, exchanging greetings, she said, "I've missed you! We have so much catching up to do."

"I know! Tell me about your conference in Ohio. I want to hear all about it!" I went to the coffee pot to pour as Marla sat on the stool on the island.

"I will. It was incredible. But first, how are you? Really?"

When I turned, mugs in hand, I saw Marla's signature expression. Her brow furrowed towards where I stood and zeroed in on me. She was one of the only people I knew with this look of genuine care. She reminded me so much of Jesus it broke my guard down.

"Honestly, it's been really hard lately. We've reopened my sister's case, and a private investigator is handling it. I mean, I should be fine, but I am just so… I don't know. Not fine? I guess."

Marla's eyes gleamed with love, and she just nodded quietly, letting me continue.

"I guess it's just bringing up a lot of memories and feelings I thought I already dealt with." My eyes began to fill, and I blinked rapidly to displace the tears.

Marla reached across the table to place a hand over mine. "That sounds really hard, Darlene."

"It is. You know I didn't always handle Marcia's passing very well." I swatted at the tear rolling down my cheek. "I'm sorry. I didn't mean for this time to be like this. I really do want to hear about your trip," I said, drying my cheek and taking a sip of coffee.

"Our friendship is about more than just the good moments. I am here for you however you need me, especially in the hard times. You know that." Marla patted my hand again before retreating and sipping her coffee, too.

"Ugh, I know…" I groaned. "I just hate feeling like this. I've worked so hard over the years to move on that I get discouraged when these feelings come back."

"You know, I almost wonder if this was a divine appointment—our time together. Because this conference I went to was all about inner healing and God's forgiveness."

I blew out a breath. "Lord knows I need more of that."

"Would it be okay if I share about what they taught us and see if any of it resonates with you?"

"Of course. Let's move to the couch." I led us through the kitchen to the living room. On the fireplace mantle was Marcia's senior photo. Even though it was faded, her blue eyes still glittered beautifully through the glass.

"Your sister was beautiful," Marla said, following my eyes.

"She was." That's what broke my heart: how hard it still was to remember to use the correct tense. Everything about Marcia was past tense. The grief grabbed at my heart again and I fought to turn from her picture so I could focus on Marla.

"Tell me more about inner healing," I prompted.

So Marla spent the better part of an hour sharing the lessons she received and how God brought healing to our wounded places. She also shared about her own journey through pain and depression and how her pastor met her where she was at with love—in her own living room!

She explained that inner healing was more about letting Jesus into those dark and painful parts of our story consciously and giving him the green light to bring healing to them. She explained repentance and surrender, giving God control of our thoughts and feelings, and how to make powerful faith statements that aligned with Scripture.

Everything she explained felt so much like common sense. I couldn't understand how I hadn't heard it all before. The longer she shared, the more my eyes pricked with tears. By the time she finished, I knew I needed her help to access the healing she described.

"Marla, I have been praying for years for God to heal this hurt. And I feel like this might be his way of answering. Can you pray for me?"

Marla's eyes glistened with the beginning of tears. "Of course. I'll pray, and then I have a couple of questions for you."

I shut my eyes, and she laid a hand on my shoulder.

"Dear Heavenly Father, we come before you now to ask for your help and guidance towards healing. Lord, you see our innermost being and are aware of every struggle we carry. We thank you that the Word tells us that you are a merciful, and healing God who longs to take away our burdens. So, we believe that you want to bring Darlene healing today. I pray that you would open her heart to your healing touch and lift the heavy burden of grief today. In Jesus' name, amen."

"Amen," I uttered.

"Darlene, with your eyes closed, I want you to ask Jesus, 'What is it you want me to surrender?'"

I prayed the question in my heart. I'd never asked God a simple question and waited for an answer before, so I wasn't sure what to expect. A resounding sense of understanding filled my mind. It was the guilt and grief of losing my sister. I felt like God's spirit was inviting me to surrender it. I told Marla.

"Would you like to give that to Jesus?" she asked in a voice so sweet and timid.

I nodded as tears began to roll down my cheeks. The weight of all the years of guilt and fears built around the trauma of losing her was so heavy; I was crushed beneath it. Day and night, no matter how much I distracted myself—the pressure always came back for me. I had begged God for decades just to take it away. It had never occurred to me that he was waiting for me to surrender it to him.

I cried harder as a wave of relief began to fill my chest. It reminded me of John 3:5, where Jesus asks a man who had been sick for a long time, "Do you want to be well?" It seems evident that in asking for his healing, he wanted to be well, but for those accustomed to long-term emotional turmoil such as grief, sometimes we feel that rejecting our grief is rejecting the very thing that is keeping our loved one alive. With Marla's assistance, I knew I was more than ready to let go and move through my grief with God rather than trying to endure it on my strength alone.

"This process is like peeling back layers of an onion. Don't be surprised if there are things you thought you 'already dealt with' that God brings back up to bring healing. God's Holy Spirit will unravel things just as he means to."

I nodded again with my eyes closed. Marla pressed a tissue into my hand, and I blew my nose. She led me to pray through a couple more questions about what Jesus wanted to give me or what he wanted me to surrender, and each time, I was amazed to experience God's reply in my heart. The wave of peace that came after each burden I surrendered had me in awe. Years of struggling with anger, denial, control, disordered thinking, and more dropped off me in a moment, and I felt the healing balm of that surrender as it took place.

After my tears had quieted, Marla changed the topic of prayer. "Darlene, I want you to picture Jesus' cross. When he died on the cross for you and me, all of our sins were nailed to that cross with him. What are some things you need to nail to that cross, figuratively speaking? Let's ask Jesus."

I prayed again quietly in my heart: *Jesus, what things do I need to nail to the cross?*

His response was immediate and unexpected. Unforgiveness. I drew back, perplexed. Then, a Bible verse sprang to mind. Matthew 6:14-15 says, "For if you forgive other people when they sin against you, your heavenly Father will also forgive you. But if you do not forgive others their sins, your Father will not forgive your sins."

I knew, deep in my heart, that God was convicting me of all the unforgiveness I had stored up. I was angry at the person who took Marcia away from me, at Marcia for moving to Georgia, at my parents for driving her away and not getting her back, and most of all, angry at myself for not being a better sister when I had the chance. The weight of the anger was crushing and toxic, and it was finally time to let it go.

I took a steadying breath. "God wants me to leave my anger and unforgiveness at the cross."

"Are you ready to do that?"

I imagined what life would look like without all of that anger. Would sadness or another negative emotion replace it? How would I stay afloat? The anger felt like a protector in the storm and even, at times, like the only thing keeping me afloat. But then I pictured Jesus walking on the water toward me. Like Peter in Matthew 14, my attempts to stay above water kept me drowning. I knew I needed to take the mercy Jesus offered.

He could pull me out of this.

"Yes."

Marla led me through a prayer of repentance. She helped me let go of my unforgiveness and anger against my loved ones and God. She gave me the safe space I needed to work through each person I was angry with. Name by name, I let each one go, feeling lighter and lighter.

When I finished forgiving every last person I could think of—the newspaper editor, the nosey nurse at work, the anorexic client who triggered me—I took a deep breath. I felt like a new person, weightless and clear-minded.

I relished the feeling for a moment, and when I opened my eyes, Marla was crying. "What is it?"

"Nothing. Jesus is just so beautiful. I am honored to be here with you right now witnessing this."

Her tears and genuine love made me cry again, this time out of gratitude. I embraced her in a hug.

After a moment, she pulled away. "Let me pray to close this time."

"Jesus, I want to thank you for my friend. Thank you for the healing work you have done in her heart today. We praise you because you are the Great Physician, and we can trust you with our hearts. Thank you for lifting her burdens and easing her pain. You are glorious and magnificent, and we love you, Jesus. Amen."

"Amen."

"Marla, you don't even know what an answer to prayer this is…" I trailed off, shaking my head.

Marla just smiled at me and sat back against the couch.

chapter 16

"This time, I want us to start with a new question for God." Marla smiled at me as we sat back on the couch together.

It had been two weeks since she'd first prayed for me, and I felt lighter than I had in years. The image of nailing my unforgiveness to the cross had me weeping in the days following but made a permanent change in my heart for the better.

"Okay." I smiled nervously. I knew there was nothing to fear, but baring your soul is still such a vulnerable act regardless of how close you are to the person asking.

"Let me pray for us, and then we'll get started."

I let my eyes fall close and reminded myself to take a deep breath. I was safe in my own home, and I was safe with God.

Marla prayed over us and over my fears and worries, and I felt God's presence enter the room with us. It was a precious moment of peace that felt like a weighted blanket settling over me. *The Lord is my comforter*, I thought with a smile. I knew I could do anything with him close by—I could face any obstacle if he held my hand.

"All right, so I want you to stay in this moment with God and ask him this question. 'God, where were you in the midst of Marcia's death?'"

My heart stuttered for only a moment before God's love embraced me. It was the very question I hurled at God in anger time after time in the weeks and months after Marcia's funeral. Rationally, I knew God could handle my true feelings with love and understanding, but a small part of my heart felt like a child standing before her father in shame at this prompting.

Squeezing my eyes closed tighter, I willed myself to pray the question. *God, where were you in the midst of Marcia's death?*

I waited for a reply, despite how wholly unfamiliar it felt compared to the way I grew up praying. The moments ticked by, and unbelief taunted me from the edge of my mind. *He's never answered before; what do you expect now?*

I shut out the enemy's voice and focused on trusting the Lord to give me peace or to reveal the answer to me like he did last time.

Instead, a memory came to mind.

It was the third night in a row I awoke to hear my father crying in the dark. News of Marcia's death was still so fresh that we were all raw and reeling from the loss. It seemed to be taking its toll, especially on my father.

I crept from my bed and tiptoed down the hall to listen at their door. My father's words were garbled in his tears and bed sheets. Mother lulled him with the same rhythmic *shush-shush* she used on all us kids.

It broke my heart to hear my parents so devastated. They didn't deserve this! As I returned to my room, I vowed to myself that I would remain strong for them; I wouldn't put them through any more pain.

The next morning, we arose slowly and went about our various routines on autopilot. I was still out of school on bereavement and floated from room to room in a stupor of grief. And that's when I heard Father's mumbling. My heart quickened at the sound—it was what I had become accustomed to hearing in the middle of the night, not in broad daylight. I became worried about his mental state hearing it now. I froze where I was in the living room watching TV and gazed over my shoulder. There in the dining room, Father sat at the table, hugging my mother's waist, struggling through his broken pain.

"What if she wasn't saved? How can we be sure?" he wailed.

The sound shook me to my core, the words rattling in my brain. We were pastors' kids. We were all saved, weren't we?

"I have to see her again in heaven, Ella Mae. I have to!" he sobbed.

I didn't understand his fear until a thought dawned on me. Was Marcia not saved? Is that why she was always acting out?

Now, this new thought that my sister might not be saved wiggled into my mind and began to take root, disturbing all the memories I had of her a moment before. What did it mean if she wasn't saved? That we would never see her again? The questions came faster and faster until I couldn't handle them any longer. I ran off to my room and shut the door.

No matter what I was going through, my parents were going through something worse. I could be strong for them. I put some music to drown out the thoughts I couldn't handle and reorganized my vinyls in alphabetical order.

Later that night, my father's sobs woke me again. I turned over, ready to roll out of bed to check on him when they stopped. I paused, waiting to hear them start up again. But they didn't.

Now, for a different reason, I found myself creeping down the hallway to their door.

"Ella Mae, do you see that white light? Look, it's right there!" Father exclaimed, the bed creaking around him.

"Ned, what light? I don't see anything." Her voice trembled, and I could hear her worry.

"It's right there! Oh, it's beautiful, Ella Mae." The pain in my father's voice was gone. It was light and moony, almost like he was in a dream.

"Ned, I'm concerned. Let me check your temperature."

With my ear pressed to the door, I heard Mother rooted around in the bedside table for the thermometer.

"Stop, I don't want to miss this," Father said.

"No, Ned, something isn't right. I'm going to call Rosemary."

At that, I ran back down the hall to my room. Hiding behind my door so my mother wouldn't see me as she left the bedroom to go to the phone hanging on the wall in the kitchen, I listened carefully. It was faint, but I could still hear the commotion.

"Rosemary, I am so sorry to call so late, but it's Ned. Can you come right now? I'm afraid he's having a stroke."

A few minutes later, there was a knock at our front door so light that I almost missed it. Mother was already at the door and flung it open, ushering our neighbor Rosemary in. Rosemary was older now, but she had been a nurse her whole life. Mother often called her when we got sick or if she had questions about food safety. Rosemary was like a grandmother to Marcia and me.

"He's in here," Mother said, coming down the hall. "He's been saying that he sees a white light."

"I brought some things. Here." She paused, and I imagined the medical tote bag she carried. What was in it at this late hour? "Hey, Ned, it's Rosemary. I'm just going to check your blood pressure, okay?"

I waited at the door in my room, cracking it open ever so quietly to hear better. After a long moment of silence, I heard the hiss of the blood pressure cuff let out.

"124 over 77." The ripping velcro partially obscured Rosemary's voice. "It's within normal range."

"Do you see that white light, Rose?" my father asked again feverishly.

"Why don't you just lay down, Ned, and get some rest."

"I'll be right back, Ned." Mother shushed over him and followed Rosemary out to the front door.

I eased my door closed again and listened closely.

"Thank you for coming over in the middle of the night. I'm sorry to bother you for nothing."

"Well, it's good you did. You never know and can never be too safe. Just keep an eye on him. I'm going to assume the stress of recent events is getting to him. The shock and emotions are probably disturbing his sleep. Make sure he's staying hydrated, eating, and getting the rest he needs, and he should be fine."

As the door closed behind Rosemary, I didn't hear anything else come from my parents' room that night.

The following day, my father was a changed man. When I emerged from my room, he was whistling while making pancakes.

"Good morning, sweetheart. Pancake?"

"Sure?" I looked around for Mom. What was going on?

"How'd you sleep?" He set a plate before me with two pancakes drizzled in maple syrup.

"Not great… How did you sleep?" That was the real question here.

"Amazing. The Lord encountered me last night! Marcia made it. She's with the Lord. I just know it." He beamed at me before turning back to the griddle.

My hands froze, fork and knife hovering over the breakfast plate. Mom breezed into the kitchen, her beige dress perfectly in place, like everything was back to normal now.

"Mom?" I asked.

She turned around, and I saw the bags under her eyes. She smiled with her mouth, but her eyes hung low, tired.

"What's going on?"

"Your father had what he believes is a visitation from the Lord."

"I have." He looked at us over his shoulder. "God has given us a beautiful gift of peace, knowing that Marcia is in heaven with him. I don't need anything else now. I have what I need."

Mother sighed and smiled at me before crossing through to the dining room.

Nov. 18, 1996

Dear Marcia;

Ten years ago today a vicious, devil, killer took your life who will some day have his reward in hell for . He may never meet judgement on earth, but He will when standing before God.

We miss you dearly and think of you every day. Some day we will see you again in heaven where evil can never enter in to separate us again. We will have you for all eternity in a wonderful place called Heaven. God care for you until we see again.

Love
Mother + Dad, 1996.

chapter 17

"God, where were you in the midst of Marcia's death?" I prayed quietly.

The memory played through and ended on my father's face. The look of complete serenity was upon him. I remembered that he had an inexplicable amount of peace after wrestling through that painful season.

When I opened my eyes, a small tear trailed down my cheek. I filled Marla in on what had happened and shared the memory of my father with her.

Her own eyes began to fill with tears. "That's so beautiful," she breathed.

"You know, that just reminded me of a time when we were kids and had to accompany my father to a funeral at the church. It wasn't for anyone we knew, but it was a family in the community. I remember watching my father fix his tie in the mirror before leaving, and he was struggling. I asked him what was wrong, and he told me that doing a funeral for someone who wasn't saved was excruciating. As a minister, my father knew what that meant.

"I never understood what my father's late-night sobs were really about until now."

"You were just a kid. How could you have known?" Marla consoled me.

"Right." I nodded, accepting the truth and pushing back the creeping guilt I felt. "It just breaks my heart to realize that's what he was so worried about."

"But God…" Marla prompted, reminding me that wasn't where the story ended.

"*But God.* You're right, God was there. He was our family's comforter during that time. He gave my father the assurance he needed. I could never see that until now." I rubbed my hand over my face. I felt so much lighter, but there were still unresolved emotions rumbling inside.

"What are you feeling, Darlene?"

"I'm not sure. I still feel guilty for some reason. I mean, I feel better, but it's almost like there's still something blocking me. Does that make sense?"

"Yes. It does. There was actually something you said earlier that I want to bring back up. In the memory, you said it broke your heart to hear your parents so devastated, and you vowed to be strong for them and not put them through any pain. Do you remember that?"

I nodded. That's exactly how I felt—I promised to make things better for them.

"Darlene, this promise you made was unhealthy for a child. There was no way you could protect them from the unknown. I believe you stepped into a role you were never meant to do: to parent your parents. And I think that's actually where you shut down your ability to effectively process your own experiences, leaving you stuck in toxic places unable to heal."

My eyes pricked once more with tears. Every word she said was hitting its target. I could barely breathe, let alone nod.

"It's important that we replace this promise with some truth from scripture. Did God tell you to be strong for your parents? To make sure you never put them through pain? No. What does God say instead?"

She paused, waiting for me, but my mind was buzzing frantically from the storm inside my chest. She continued for me.

"God tells us that *his* grace is sufficient for us and that *his* power is made perfect in *our* weakness. You don't have to be strong for anyone, Darlene. Your job is to lean on the Lord in your weakness. You're allowed to struggle too. Your pain matters to God, and he's big enough to carry all your grief as well as your parents!"

I broke, the walls around my heart crumbling down and the sobs tumbling through. Marla sat close by, letting me cry it all out—all the pain I held back, every emotion I held behind an ever-weakening veil because I was afraid no one could handle it. I was so scared that this pain would overflow like a dam breaking me and that I wouldn't be able to stop hurting others. I had already witnessed how grief clawed its way through our family. I was terrified mine would do the same.

"His grace is sufficient for you, Darlene. Let it all go into the loving hands of our God," Marla whispered this gently to me as I grieved from a place I'd never been released from. Deep, guttural cries rolled out of me, cracking my face and swelling my eyes.

"God's got you. He will bear your pain," she continued to assure me. Each truth she spoke was precisely what my weary heart needed. I had heard these truths before in church, but I never thought they could reach the depths of places I was hiding. I don't know why, but it just never connected until that day when Marla pointed to it. It was crucial to this part of my healing to have someone I trusted speak God's truth directly to me in a loving way.

Minutes ticked by, and the well of tears began to dry. My stomach ached from the heaving tears, and Marla began to rub small circles on my back to soothe me.

"You were never meant to carry all of this alone, Darlene. Are you ready to nail your burdens to the cross and surrender once and for all to Jesus?"

I took a deep, cleansing breath that shuddered on its way out, but I nodded. "I'm ready."

Marla reminded me how to pray through surrendering this pain to Jesus, and I followed her steps, visualizing the cross, seeing my sin and shame and grief all upon Jesus' shoulder, and seeing Jesus die and come to life again, leaving all I let go of in the grave he rose from.

I felt the relief immediately. My burden was truly lifted.

"Only God..." I whispered, mesmerized.

"Only God." Marla smiled, eyes bright.

chapter 18

More than three months had passed, and there was no movement on the case. I tried to keep myself busy so I wouldn't bug Morgan, looking for answers she couldn't provide. She warned me that lulls like this would be normal and that cold cases don't get solved overnight. But despite that fact, I had warmed to the idea of closure.

Readying myself for work one morning, I heard the familiar ding of a Facebook message. Turning away from the bathroom mirror, I grabbed my phone.

It was Morgan.

"I requested the entire case files for both Marcia Burkett and Dawn Cobeen again. I was told 'Gwinnett County has reviewed its files and has determined there are no responsive documents to your request.' Which we know is a lie due to documents I have already obtained."

After months of waiting for the county office to send a reply, *this* is what they go with? A bald-faced lie?

I was so angry I could spit.

"Seriously?" I jabbed my fingers on the screen, punching out a reply. "How can they do that? Can they even do that?"

"I'm going to try again and let you know what results I get.."

I tried not to let it ruin my day, but my mind couldn't help but drift back towards disappointment. Every time it seemed like I was healing, something came to rip the bandage off and reopen the wound. It was exhausting.

☙

A week later, I had just finished stuffing groceries into my car when I heard my phone's alert. I figured it was Matt letting me know he was on his way home, so I took my time shuffling the cart back to the return.

It wasn't until I got home that I remembered the message. Putting the car in park, I pulled out the phone from my purse.

It was another update from Morgan.

"After sending in yet another request, I was told, 'I was unable to locate any reports in our system. The case numbers listed are not Gwinnett County Police case numbers.' Which, again, is a lie. Because we already have a file from their station and have talked to people there previously who have confirmed the case."

"This is just nonsense, Morgan. How do you put up with it?" A small part of me felt like I was sixteen again, lost and broken. The crack in my heart widened, and I fought to think of Jesus instead of the despair calling my name.

Three little dots appeared and boggled for a while—so long that I shoved my phone back in my purse and lugged the groceries in. Starting dinner, I fervently checked the screen, needing her response, feeling untethered without it.

As the evening faded, I gave up waiting for a message and turned my phone off.

Before bed, I crawled onto my knees and asked God for help. I had started practicing waiting for God to reply when I prayed, just like Marla had shown me. He didn't always answer or I didn't always understand it, but I tried anyway.

I felt a tug on my heart like conviction as I thought of the feeling that gripped my heart as I waited for Morgan's message. I sighed. I wasn't putting my trust in God so much as I was turning to Morgan and the world's justice system. The verse from Psalms 118 came to mind: "It is better to trust in the LORD Than to put confidence in man."

Thank you, Lord, for leading me and pulling me close. I'm sorry for allowing fear to turn my heart away from you. Help me to trust you when times get hard, and the world's system fails me. I don't want to forget you and all that you've done for me. Please help me.
Amen

☙

A week later, Morgan sent another message.
08/16/2022
"I requested Marcia's case file again and was told, 'Upon further review of your request, I have discovered that due to the age of this case, your request for records has to go through a different department. The case numbers assigned to older homicide cases have a different format than the original GCPD case number that may have been assigned.'"

I didn't reply. I couldn't find the energy to bring myself to care. If they weren't going to care, then neither was I.

☙

The next update came two weeks later.
08/31/2022
"I received an email regarding my request that was denied on 08/07/2022, stating that if I paid them $44.13, then they would release the records to me. I made the payment and was only given the incident report, which was the very first document I received back in 2019 (three years ago), for free."

That one made me mad. How unjust and corrupt has our system become in thirty or forty years?!

Three months later—
11/20/2023

"I requested the Fire/EMS records specifically for Marcia's case. They told me it would cost $50.00 just to search for them, but they do not believe records go that far back.

"I requested the Medical Examiners records for Marcia. They told me there were no records on file through the Medical Examiner's office. I am assuming this is because she went as a Jane Doe for so long, but I do know the file has to exist somewhere out there.

"I requested to see if there were any arrest records for Marcia in Gwinnett County, to which they stated no."

When I got this last message from Morgan, I picked up the phone to call her.

"What is going on?"

"The local police department has been quite unresponsive regarding responding to my inquiries. All I've been told is, 'This is an open investigation, nothing can be released.'"

"But that's not even true—they have given us things in the past!"

"Yeah. Sometimes, they gave me a report for free; other times, they charged me forty dollars for the same report. And now they're saying that they will require a 'search fee' to even look for documents that may not even exist."

"Morgan..." I groaned, and I let my head drop into my hand.

"This, unfortunately, is what happens to so many people every single day. The police have what they need, but they refuse to give it to us. Sometimes, after pressing them for a while, they give in.

"But this has yet to happen in Marcia's case, unfortunately. Sometimes, it seems like they don't care that a human was murdered. Or that they don't want us to find anything out. It's like this is just a job for them.

"I get it, the cops need to make a living too, but just because a murder happened in 1986 and not 2020 doesn't mean that the investigation can just be put on pause.

"Like I said before, if stuff like this keeps happening, it makes people think that they will not get caught for committing crimes, therefore increasing the homicide rates."

I found myself nodding along to her impassioned speech. I didn't have any words. Her frustration echoed everything I thought along the way.

Don't the police care?

I know they have a job to do, but... I lost my sister, and I desperately need closure.

"I—" I sighed audibly.

"I'm not going to quit, Darlene. I'm going to keep fighting."

Jesus,
How did you endure the pain of loss? How did you endure Judas' betrayal? Better yet, how did you endure the betrayal of the Pharisees and Pontius Pilate? The Pharisees were

supposed to be on your side as the religious leaders of that time, but instead, they plotted to kill you. And Pontius Pilate was supposed to be the city's leader—the government, the voice of justice and law and fairness—and instead of setting you free, he washed his hands of guilt and let you be led away to slaughter.

How do you handle this level of disappointment in the system that was created to be trusted? How do you find hope to keep going?

God, I really need you to speak wisdom and peace into my heart.

Matthew 27:19-26 NIV

While Pilate was sitting in the judge's seat, his wife sent him this message: "Don't have anything to do with that innocent man, for I have suffered a great deal today in a dream because of him."

But the chief priests and the elders persuaded the crowd to ask for Barabbas and to have Jesus executed.

"Which of the two do you want me to release to you?" asked the governor.

"Barabbas," they answered.

"What shall I do, then, with Jesus who is called the Messiah?" Pilate asked.

They all answered, "Crucify him!"

"Why? What crime has he committed?" asked Pilate.

But they shouted all the louder, "Crucify him!"

When Pilate saw that he was getting nowhere but that instead an uproar was starting, he took water and washed his hands in front of the crowd. "I am innocent of this man's blood," he said. "It is your responsibility!"

All the people answered, "His blood is on us and on our children!"

Then he released Barabbas to them. But he had Jesus flogged and handed him over to be crucified.

Luke 23:32-24 NIV

Two other men, both criminals, were also led out with him to be executed. When they came to the place called the Skull, they crucified him there, along with the criminals—one on his right, the other on his left. Jesus said, "Father, forgive them, for they do not know what they are doing." And they divided up his clothes by casting lots.

Thank you, Jesus, for speaking to me through your Word. Thank you, Lord, that you have experienced every sort of pain and grief that we have here on earth. Thank you for showing me how you handled it. Even when you were innocent and handed over to your accusers, you chose forgiveness. Give me the same strength to choose forgiveness towards the police, the investigators, and anyone involved in withholding Marcia's information. Thank you, Lord.

In Jesus' name, I pray,
Amen

chapter 19

Christmas Eve, 2023

As we sat, gathered around the dinner table, Matt at the head, our two children and my mother in the middle, and myself at the other end, I took a deep breath. It was our first year without my father. While my heart ached that he was gone, I couldn't be more relieved that he had found peace in the years since Marcia's passing.

It had been three years since Marcia's case was "reopened" by Morgan, and it had been three years of struggling, processing grief, and finding healing in profound ways. I never thought I would be where I am now, strangely at peace with the loss of my sister.

Out of the corner of my eye, the twinkling lights on the tree pulled my attention from the fuss of everyone settling in for Christmas dinner. One of the ornaments was a beautiful mosaic of broken stained glass. I watched as it danced in the blinking lights.

I have loved Christmas ever since I was a girl. That special family buzz of having everyone gathered together for a time was meaningful to me, but a pang of loss reminded me that my sister wasn't here. She would never be here for another Christmas again. Even though I had grieved this loss before, this painful reminder that she was missing sprang up every year. Grief was like that. Sometimes, it was a heavy load on my back, and some days, it was just a pebble in my shoe. Today, it was a manageable pebble but a painful reminder nonetheless.

The table shifted ever so slightly, bringing my eyes back to Matt's. He beamed at me, then at the kids. We were both excited that they were home for the holidays and that we would open presents with them after dinner. Even though they were older, I still couldn't wait to see their faces light up with excitement.

Matt cleared his throat, getting everyone's attention; he was ready to pray and start dinner. We all bowed our heads as he said grace. As he did, I let my mind get stuck on the word grace.

What was grace? What did it really mean? The scriptures tell us that God gave us grace abundantly. I let my mind dwell on it long after the amen was said and the potatoes were passed.

I think grace is about God's presence and strength in every aspect of our lives. He surrounds us when we are weak and fills in the gaps in our strength so we can get through. Grace is the essence of himself, the power of his presence working wonders in our lives to accomplish the impossible while showing us his clear hand in our survival. It may look different in someone else's life, but this is how it looked in mine.

I can see God's grace more clearly in the face of my many questions.

Why did Marcia have to die so young?

Why did it happen to her and not me?

Why did this happen to our family at all?

Why aren't the police doing more to find the guy who did this?

Will we ever have justice, and when?

Why don't we have more answers?

Why… Why… Why…

There aren't any cookie-cutter answers to these questions. I have to settle myself into a reality that may never hold the answers I seek in this lifetime. But even though I don't have the answers to the unknown, I have a faithful God to carry me through.

God asks us to trust him in the midst of the unknown, to lean on his grace and mercy for us. I know again, even at this moment, that God is asking me to trust that he's here with me and accept his grace is sufficient.

I handled the vegetables as they were passed to me, scooping some onto my plate when my daughter looked over at me.

"Mom, did anything more come from Marcia's case?" She reached for a cup of water to wash down the casserole.

I paused before sighing heavily. I didn't particularly want to have this conversation in front of my mother. The kids had been away at school when Morgan started looking into the case, and I never mentioned it to my parents to avoid getting their hopes up. But earlier this week, my daughter had found a newspaper clipping of Marcia's obituary while we were searching for Mom's old address book.

And now they were all looking at me.

"No, honey," I cleared my throat. "Morgan will let us know if she finds anything out, but I don't suspect anything more will come to light." I kept my eyes on her, hoping it wouldn't drag my mother into a negative space.

"I'm sorry, Mom, that must be really hard."

I looked down at my plate, considering how to steer the conversation to its end. I haven't fully allowed the people in my family or workplace to understand how much work and faith it has taken me to get to where I am. I felt more than ready to point towards the redemptive work of the Lord if I could.

"You know, honey, it really is. But God is so good to us despite this broken mess. He didn't make this happen, but he is working it out for good."

"I don't understand," she shook her head, "how could anything good come from Aunt Marcia's death?"

I looked again at the tree, that same ornament catching my eye. "You know how mosaics are made? You have to break beautiful glass pieces in order to create something new. The process seems a little crude to ruin a perfectly good work of art. But what you make with it is something one-of-a-kind, beautiful and inspiring. Where it's been fused, it's stronger. The light shines through and refracts in many more directions now than it could before. The crazy thing is that mosaics end up being more valuable than the pieces they originated from.

"That's how it is when God steps into our messes—he picks up the broken pieces and makes something beautiful."

She seemed to accept that answer with a careful nod.

Something in my heart shifted. It hit me—just how true what I'd said was. I thought about how much time I spent pretending I felt nothing and living in denial with this grief—and I could have spent many more years stuck there—until I realized how little it was helping me to move on truly. The truth I spoke about the mosaic hit home as I explained it to the table: when you let the light shine through your broken places, you point people to the Healer.

I had kept silent for so long, hiding the depths of my loss, even lying about it to people who asked. It never dawned on me that sharing about it was my calling. It didn't occur to me that this was the way forward and would give God the most glory.

God never called me to hide. He called me to be a light. He was just waiting for me to see that.

to help

If you or someone you know may have more information about the cold cases relating to Marcia Burkett or Dawn Cobeen, please contact one of the following. Thank you!

The Gwinnett County Police Department (GA, USA)
Phone: 770-822-8000

Morgan Beaird, Private Investigator at BWI Investigations Forensics (TN, USA)
Phone: (615) 646-0860
Email: morgan@berryinv.com

victim's resources

If you or someone you know is a victim of a violent crime, assault, or trafficking, please know that help is available.

The Victim Connect Resource Center
The Victim Connect Resource Center (VCRC) is a weekday phone, chat, and text-based referral helpline for all victims of crime in the United States.
Phone: 855-484-2846
Website: https://www.victimconnect.org

The National Center for Victims of Crime
Website: https://victimsofcrime.org/

The National Sexual Assault Hotline
Phone: 800-656-4673

The National Human Trafficking Hotline
Phone: 888-373-7888

The National Domestic Violence Hotline
Website: 1-800-799-SAFE

The National Suicide Prevention Lifeline
Behavioral and mental health crisis services are now available through 988. Individuals can call, text, or chat with 988.
Phone: 1-800-273-8255

Citizens Against Physical, Sexual and Emotional Abuse (CAPSEA)
24/7 Confidential Hotline serving Elk County, PA and Cameron County, PA.
Elk County Hotline: 814-772-1227
Cameron County Hotline: 814-486-0952

Community Action, Inc.
Primarily Serving Clarion and Jefferson Counties, Pennsylvania.
Website: https://www.jccap.org
For All Domestic Violence Emergencies: 1-800-598-3998
For Homeless Emergencies: 1-800-598-3998

see something,
SAY SOMETHING

"Every year, at least 5,000 killers get away with murder. More than 285,000 Americans have perished in unsolved homicides committed since 1980—more than the combined death toll of all U.S. military actions since World War II."[1]

"4,400 unidentified bodies are recovered every year. It is referred to as "The Nation's Silent Mass Disaster"."[2]

Help put an end to violence.
How to submit a tip to the Say Something program:
1. Say Something website: SaySomething.net
2. Say Something mobile app: App Store | Google Play
3. Say Something hotline: 1-844-5-SAY NOW

---

1 https://www.murderdata.org/
2 https://www.namus.gov//

grief resources

If you or someone you know is suffering with the loss of a loved one here are some resources to support you during grief.

National Organization of Parents Of Murdered Children
Phone: 888-818-7662

Parents of Murdered Children
Website: https://www.pomc.org/

Siblings of Murdered Siblings
Website: https://siblingsofmurderedsiblings.org/

word from the author:
THE STORY BEHIND THE BOOK

This book is about the loss of my precious sister, Marcia, who was murdered. This has been a 37-year-old journey.

I never dreamed this book would come to fruition as the many decades of repressed anger, hurt, and sadness that I continued to wrap myself around me were like a nice cozy security blanket, which had become my "comfort zone" for many years—many *decades*—of my life. It was one of the deepest, most treasured secrets that I had learned to keep safely tucked away in one of the four chambers of my heart, only allowing others to have a sneak peek at my own discretion.

I had an encounter back in 2018 with a dear friend, Marla, who helped me release many deeply rooted, repressed emotions that I was harboring in my heart. I knew what I had always done in the past wasn't a healthy outlet, but I didn't know how to release the pain. I also realized that when I had to face the pain, it meant releasing those difficult memories of the trauma, and I didn't want to release that ugly monster.

When you expose your pain to others, you never realize that there is always a possibility that you can help them heal as well. Exposing my pain would make me vulnerable and transparent. I didn't want their sympathy or their questions, which often led to a deeper well of pain. I wanted the pain to stop at all costs. I wanted to numb it. For me, refusing to remember that frozen moment in time was numbing it all!

Sharing your trauma with others means that you have to take a step back and recall those dark memories that drag you back into the dark hole. That hole allowed me not to feel such raw emotion or experience extreme sadness, helplessness, overwhelming grief, and depression all over again.

༄

One Sunday in 2022 at my church, I decided to ask God to stretch my faith and make me uncomfortable, never imagining what that would look like, only that I wanted to step out.

At this point, I had already personally met Morgan, who had opened Pandora's box of memories whenever we would speak on the phone. I knew I had a higher purpose in this life, and pursuing God's direction was the ultimate goal. What if only one person could be reached through reading this book, and what would that look like for them? Could they help others? Isn't that the goal that God wants for us? After all, the thing that caused me to step out of my comfort zone could provide comfort to others. I understood God's mission, and that was to reach the lost and help them understand that no matter what kind of trauma or grief you encounter, you are never alone. God is always with you! I am often reminded of the beautiful following Bible verses:

- Psalm 147:3 - He heals the brokenhearted and binds up their wounds.
- Philippians 2:4 Let each of you look not only to his own interests but also to the interests of others.

In September 2023, Morgan reached out to me and asked me if I would be interested in summarizing some great memories of Marcia to help her understand who she was on a deeper level. I informed Morgan that I would think about this and would sit down in a week to attempt to remember those memories for her. I managed to type up four pages of beautiful memories for Morgan.

After re-reading these pages over and over in my head, I decided to toss the idea around to a friend of mine named Katie. I had met Katie about five years prior through a mutual friend. Katie attended the church where my father pastored in Dubois, PA. She had Bible studies at the church a few years ago, which I attended. I decided to inquire about her recently established book company that she started in 2021. Katie stated that she would be interested in meeting with me about her company to see if I was ready to have my story published. We scheduled a meeting on October 4, 2023, at the local coffee shop in town. Katie relayed all the information about moving forward with a book if that was what I decided to do. I informed her that I would need a week to speak to God for clarity regarding the direction he wanted me to pursue. I felt moved to push forward to share this story to help others. As I wrestled with the next best step, I continued to feel God moving me toward telling my story in the hopes that it would help others with similar journeys. It was scary to step from a safe place and out into the relative unknowns of vulnerability.

As I continued to pray about the correct decision, I remembered how much Marcia loved the color purple. I thought about how amazing it would be if I could find a purple flower that was between the sidewalk cracks. I have attuned my eye to any signs that show how beauty can survive through adversity and even grow. I found a few photos on Google of several purple flowers that I decided to save as I continued to question whether or not I would move forward.

On October 9, 2023, I met a friend at the same coffee shop where I had met Katie a few days prior. It was on a busy Monday morning. A peculiar-looking man wearing a brown bomber jacket with numbers written on a black Sharpie all over it continued to walk in and out of the coffee shop. He had a bewildered look on his face. I asked him if he was in line. He quickly replied, "Oh, no, I am outside playing my guitar as I recently lost my job, and I found the coolest thing around the corner, so I wanted to show these workers the photo." This man then showed me the photo, and to my surprise, there it was—a beautiful purple petunia growing in the sidewalk cracks. Trying to hold back the tears, I asked this stranger if he would mind showing me where this flower was found. As I left the shop and walked around the corner, it was all of its loveliness there. I stood in utter amazement. Who would have ever imagined a purple petunia in between the sidewalk cracks in October? But there it was. I took the photo with tears streaming down my face, which became the inspiration for the cover photo for this book. I then went home to talk to a friend about this event. She suddenly told me that the title of my book was a perfect name. I stated, "The December Grave" clearly does not go with a flower for the book. She then stated, "You never told me, 'The December Grave' but 'December Grace.'" I was utterly speechless at this point. *Okay, God, I am hearing you loud and clear.* This was two confirmations in one day. I still had a few more days to decide, so I continued to wait and seek God.

I decided to contact Marla to gather her thoughts. She stated that if I chose to publish this book, it would be such an inspiration to have a mother's experience of losing a child. I informed her that I had nothing pertaining to that from my mother and had rarely spoken to my mother about her experience as it always brought such immediate sadness. The following day, I decided to look for the newspaper articles of Marcia's passing. Trying to recall where I had placed the clippings, it occurred to me thirty minutes later. There, they were safely tucked away in an old RCA bag that Marcia once had many of her forty-five vinyl records inside. Above the bag was another unfamiliar bag. To my astonishment, there were three typed papers, all from my mother and her fresh memories from 1987. I was never able to recall the day Marcia was buried in Pennsylvania other than I knew it was near Easter that year in April of 1987. God once again showed me that day in my mother's typed letters, April 22, 1987. I didn't pursue God for any more clarity as all of these incidents that many would often call "just coincidences" were not coincidences. God was showing up, loud and boldly, in just a week's time frame. I emailed Katie on October 11 to confirm that I wanted to follow God's direction and pursue this story.

This book was never about me! It was to serve God and to be used by him. He used me as a vessel to help others. We aren't meant to hide our pain and struggles but to step out of our comfort zone and comfort others. Sibling grief is extremely unrecognized. When you lose a spouse, you become a widow or widower; if you lose a parent, you become an orphan, but when you lose a sibling, you just become a sibling who lost a sister or brother. You lose your past and your future when you lose that sibling. No one walked that journey with you, remembering your past while walking with you into your future.

I struggled with having a photo of myself in this book as I want no credit—only that God used me to share this story. In doing so, I pray that this book touched someone along the journey of reading it. I pray that you can help others throughout your walk of life. We all have a story to share, and what that looks like for you is up to you. If it is something you struggle with, laying it at the cross and fully surrendering can become the most freeing experience you will ever encounter in your life.

- Proverbs 3:5-6 - "Trust in the LORD with all your heart and lean not on your own understanding; in all your ways submit to him, and he will make your paths straight."

- Matthew 16:24 - "If anyone would come after me, let him deny himself and take up his cross and follow me."

I can honestly say I have had many doubts about continuing to pursue this book, as Satan has attempted to attack me from every angle. Spiritual warfare was coming in full force for many, many months upon myself and my family. However, that only validated the unseen battle that was going on. I realized that God would win this battle in the end. This was to glorify God and his purpose. Ephesians 6:12 states, "For our struggle is not against flesh and blood, but against the rulers, against the authorities, against the powers of this dark world and against the spiritual forces of evil in the heavenly realms."

I have finally been able to move forward and forgive. Letting go of the hate that was holding me in bondage and slavery for too many years allowed me to heal my heart and surrender freely what I was never meant to carry. Although Marcia's murder has not been solved, and may never be, I am finally at peace knowing that I have forgiven Marcia's murderer and I can someday look God in the eyes to hear him say, "Well done my good and faithful servant." Oh, what a beautiful sound that will be echoed throughout eternity when I come face to face with our Savior.

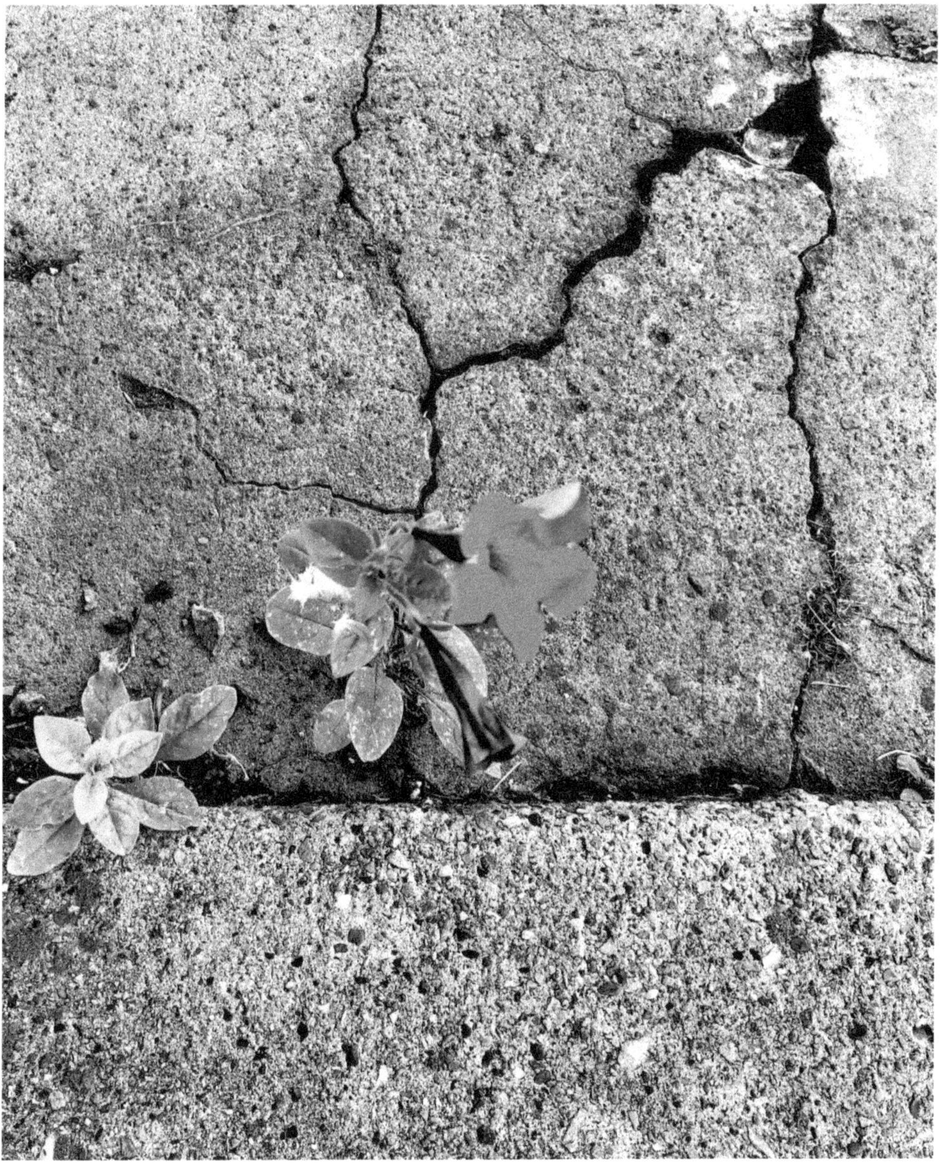

word from the author:
A PERSONAL REFLECTION ON GRIEF

As I reflect upon this thirty-eight-year-long journey through the anger, denial, and many years of overwhelming sadness, I realized that God has given me this story, despite the ugliness of it, to use it for his glory and help others. Everyone in this life struggles with pain, and if we choose to bottle that pain up and never allow it to strengthen us to help others, what is the purpose of that pain?

The petunia flower photo that I snapped off my cell phone on October 9 was a beautiful gift that God gave me. He showed me that through the broken cracks and crevices in our heart and soul, there is healing. When we allow healing to occur, beauty can grow and flourish. God was there during my storm, and despite the uphill journey that this was along the way, I can now look back and realize he never left me. He walked beside me, comforting me on the sleepless nights of sadness and tears. He was in front of me, protecting me from the dangers that the world can engulf us into. When the days were dark and I didn't know which way to go, he encompassed me with his light. God hurt even more than I had been hurting as this was his daughter, Marcia, who had been given to me for sixteen years.

What are you doing with your pain? Is it helping others? Is it encouraging others despite how ugly that story may be? We all have a story, and what we choose to do with it becomes a decision only you can make. Had someone told me that this story needed to be shared five years ago, I would have said, "You're crazy!" There is no way I could have shared this as it truly exhibits vulnerability and transparency. God showed me that this story needed to be shared to help others with grief. This story is to glorify him despite the raw ugliness of it. Just like the broken cracks, light will always illuminate and beauty will grow. Allow your beauty to help others. In the end, that is all we have to look back and realize that we did the best with our story and how it helped others. Every year that Marcia's death would arrive, I used to think, "Wow, she's been gone for that many years. I now look at it as another year closer. Another year closer to seeing her. What a

grand reunion that will be.
- Psalm 147:3 - He heals the brokenhearted and binds up their wounds.

Grief is a natural response to loss, and it can be incredibly challenging. Whether you're dealing with the death of a loved one, a breakup, or any other significant loss, here are some healthy ways to cope:
1. Acknowledge Your Feelings: Allow yourself to feel the emotions associated with grief. It's normal to experience shock, anger, disbelief, guilt, and profound sadness. Don't suppress these feelings; instead, recognize them and give yourself permission to grieve.
2. Seek Support: Reach out to friends, family, or a counselor. Talking about your feelings with someone who listens and understands can be incredibly helpful. Consider joining a support group or connecting with others who have experienced similar losses.
3. Take Care of Your Physical Health:
- Prioritize sleep, nutrition, and exercise. Grief can disrupt your physical well-being, so focus on maintaining a healthy routine.
- Be patient with yourself if you're having trouble sleeping or eating. These disruptions are normal during the grieving process.
4. Express Your Feelings:
- Write in a journal or talk out loud about your emotions. Expressing your thoughts and feelings can provide relief and help you process the pain.
- Consider creative outlets like art, music, or poetry to channel your emotions.
5. Create a Daily Routine:
- Establishing a routine can provide stability during a time of upheaval. Focus on the things you can control, such as maintaining regular meals and exercise.
6. Celebrate the Life of Your Loved One:
- Remember the positive memories and moments you shared with the person you lost. Celebrate their life and the impact they had on you.

Remember that grief is a highly individual experience, and there's no right or wrong way to grieve. Be patient with yourself, seek support, and allow the healing process to unfold naturally. If needed, consider professional help or counseling to navigate through this challenging time.

grief discussion
QUESTIONS

1. What is grief to you?
2. Everybody faces a loss and pain we can't control. It's important to be able to process that pain in a healthy manner. What are some positive coping skills that assisted you through your grief?
3. How do you deal with the waves of loneliness when they hit?
4. How do you deal with not being able to see them, hug them, or reach out to them any longer?
5. When do you feel your grief the most?
6. I feel most connected with my loved one when...?
7. What list of people can you turn to for support, either in person or virtually?
8. One thing I want to remember about them is?
9. Describe a memory with your loved one that makes you laugh.
10. Is there anyone else I know going through this right now? How can we support each other?

about the author

A native of rural northwestern Pennsylvania, Darlene Gildersleeve lives with her husband, Matt, and enjoys spending time with her two adult children, Rachel and Ryan. She earned her Bachelor of Social Work degree from Roberts Wesleyan College. She is the author of her debut inspirational autobiography book, *December Grace*. Darlene has had over thirty years of working as a therapist with mental health patients and has extensive experience working through her own personal grief and loss. During her spare time, Darlene enjoys spending time outside in nature with her collie, Laddie, taking photos, and traveling to national parks in the USA with her family.

December Grace was written to assist others on their grief journey. May you find healing, forgiveness, and a way to trust in the midst of the "unknowns" of this life, especially when life turns out in the least expected way.

Milton Keynes UK
Ingram Content Group UK Ltd.
UKHW020653131124
451151UK00018B/325